As a pastor evangelist ... in the centre but is also ...ery practical and eminently readable. We urgently need to recapture a belief in evangelism and share the author's love for it.

Philip H Hacking

Bible teacher, Retired Anglican priest
past Chairman of the Keswick Convention, Sheffield

When it comes to evangelism, my heart beats with the heart of Roger Carswell. Nowhere is there such a clear and convincing case set forth for the call of the evangelist and the need for those called to answer. Your understanding of the work of the evangelist will be challenged by this book and your heart will be stirred. Surely if you are not called to be an evangelist, you will want to clear the way and support the work of those who are called. People need the Lord and God still has them on His heart. They should be on our hearts as well.

Woodrow Kroll

Former President, Back to the Bible radio and television ministry, Lincoln, Nebraska

Biblical, interesting, challenging and provocative, this book fills a huge gap, not just in contemporary Christian literature, but in the outlook of the average church. The author's heart as an evangelist is worn on his sleeve without apology, demonstrating not only a deep concern for those outside of Christ, but a contagious love for God.

Charles Price

Senior Pastor, The People's Church, Toronto

Throughout the history of God's work, evangelists have led the charge of the church into the fields of harvest. This book is a clear and compelling word to us to encourage and empower the evangelist of our day.

Joseph M. Stowell

President, Cornerstone University, Grand Rapids, Michigan

From someone who is trying to learn to do this work, I found there was gold on page after page. I thoroughly recommend this book of accumulated wisdom from years of experience.

Rico Tice

Author, *Christianity Explored*, Associate Minister, All Souls Church, London

I know Roger as a friend and evangelist and as a person who practices what he preaches. This book is greatly needed, especially in the light of Satan's strategy to destroy men and women for ministry. Please read it prayerfully with your L-plates on.

George Verwer

Founder and Former International Director of Operation Mobilisation, Kent

In recent years, we've so emphasized 'pastors and teachers' that we've almost forgotten that Ephesians 4:11 also names 'evangelists'. In this book, Roger Carswell challenges us to discover and develop evangelists in our churches. From Scripture and his own rich experience, he tells us how to do it. This book is *must* reading for all of God's people, especially leaders in local churches.

Warren W. Wiersbe

Author and Conference Speaker

A few years ago I had the privilege of meeting Roger Carswell and Benjamin, his son, who were visiting the Word of Life Bible Conference Center in Schroon, New York. I not only got to hear him preach the Word, but also had some rich opportunities for Christian fellowship with him and his terrific son.

Three things come to mind when I think of Roger Carswell. First, he is a warm, articulate expositor of the Word. Second, he has strong convictions about major issues in theology. Third, he has great charm and a British sense of humor, which I deeply appreciate. When he comes to the States to minister in various venues, he takes the initiative to call me. This is not easy, since both of us move around quite a bit with our respective ministries. I really appreciated his loyalty and his friendship the last several years. My dad, Jack Wyrtzen, was a great evangelist. He went to be with the Lord back in the spring of 1996. I miss him greatly. In so many ways I wish that he could write an endorsement for this fine book. He had a burning passion for evangelism wherever it occurred the world over. I am sure that this new work will be a motivator for up and coming young evangelists. It will also be an educational tool in helping them understand what the Scripture teaches about this lost calling and almost forgotten gift of the church.

Don Wyrtzen

Composer and Musician

And Some Evangelists

Growing your church through discovering and developing evangelists

ROGER CARSWELL

Copyright © Roger Carswell 2014

paperback ISBN 978-1-78191-519-6
epub ISBN 978-1-78191-541-7
Mobi ISBN 978-1-78191-546-2

10 9 8 7 6 5 4 3 2 1

Printed in 2014
by
Christian Focus Publications Ltd.,
Geanies House, Fearn, Ross-shire,
IV20 1TW, Scotland, UK.

www.christianfocus.com

Cover design by Daniel van Straaten

Printed by
Bell and Bain, Glasgow

Contents

Foreword *by Warren W. Wiersbe*.. 9

Preface... 11

1. Where have all the evangelists gone? 13

2. God's agenda for each generation.. 23

3. Old Testament 'evangelists' 27

4. Christ, the Evangelist.. 37

5. The Holy Spirit as an Evangelist 43

6. New Testament evangelists.. 49

7. The uniqueness of the evangelist 61

8. Biblical pictures of the evangelist... 67

9. A great cloud of witnesses 77

10. An earnest plea for evangelists 91

11. The Bible as a tool 107

12. The tract as a tool... 113

13. The children's evangelist 119

14. The message and messenger 127

15. Some contentious issues 139

16. The temptations of the evangelist 153

17. Problems, principles and parables for the evangelist...................... 169

18. 'And sow to reap':

    An exposition for evangelists, about evangelism 177

Appendix: The Amsterdam Affirmations 185

Select Bibliography... 189

Dedication

Dedicated to Paul Hinton, Jeremy Hudson, Andrew Stovell and Gus Eyre, and their wives Fiona, Sue, Judith and Wendy. Working together with them in our 'Association of Evangelists', I have grown to increasingly respect and appreciate their love for the Lord, their vision to reach others and our fellowship together.

Foreword

Is there a New Testament evangelist in your church?

I'm not referring to an itinerant evangelist who comes for a week of special meetings, as important and essential as such ministries are. I'm referring to the people in your own church who have been gifted by God to lead lost people to faith in Christ and to encourage everybody in the church family to 'do the work of an evangelist' (2 Tim. 4:5).

All of us as God's people are called to be witnesses, but some are also called to be evangelists (Eph. 4:11). Like pastors and teachers, these evangelists in local churches are called to equip the saints for the work of ministry, and that includes the ministry of evangelism. *If we expect to see expanding evangelism in the nation and the world, there must be evangelists in local churches keeping the fires burning.*

It's been my privilege to pastor three churches, and in each of these churches God gave us people who were gifted at reaching the lost with the Gospel. No matter where they went day after day, they were constrained by the Lord to share Christ and challenge sinners to trust Him. Their zeal helped to keep the ministry of evangelism healthy in the congregation as well as in the pulpit.

In this timely book, Roger Carswell gives us the biblical basis for continuous evangelism in the local church, and he backs up these instructions with examples from his own wide ministry. Roger makes it clear that the church cannot reach a lost world only through the ministry of full-time evangelists. Local churches must discover evangelists within their own congregations and commission them to help God's people do the work of evangelism better. Some of these evangelists may become full-time servants of God, but then others must take their place to keep the work of evangelism strong and fruitful in the local church.

Because of their generous missionary giving, many churches are winning more souls to Christ where the church *isn't* than where the church *is*. But the Lord commanded us to start at home – in our own Jerusalem, Judea and Samaria – and not make missions overseas a substitute for evangelism at home. Each local church is one generation short of extinction and the only way to keep the family growing is through evangelism.

Roger Carswell tells us how we can do it, and I pray that God will give this book wide exposure and great acceptance among God's people.

Warren W. Wiersbe
Author and Conference Speaker

Preface

This book is an expression of my heart. My prayer is that each chapter will be read and used to stir up Christian leaders and future evangelists to seek to encourage the gift, or do the work of the evangelist, so that we might again make inroads into areas of spiritual darkness. Only our generation can reach people of this generation with the gospel. We are under orders to 'Go into all the world and preach the gospel to every creature' (Mark 16:15). That command not only includes reaching our friends, but also all those who do not have Christian contacts, who desperately need to be confronted with Christ.

I want to thank Mr Ray Beeley of Sheffield, Mr David Harding of Milnrow, Dr Woodrow Kroll and my son Benjamin for their many helpful insights and additions to this book. And also my parents, who despite cataracts and Parkinson's disease, did such a thorough job of proof reading, especially as my computer keys do not seem to stay in the same place when I am typing. I am grateful to David Larsen, whom I have never met, but whose book, *The Evangelism Mandate* was discovered at the right time, as far as my thinking about the theme of this book was concerned. I am also indebted to Sterling W. Huston's book, *The Billy Graham Crusade Handbook*, for much of the information in the first part of chapter eight.

Dr Warren Wiersbe has been a constant encouragement to me over many years, and has particularly spurred me on and helped me in writing this book. I am grateful to him, even though he could have done a better job of writing it himself.

I am grateful, too, to my wife Dot and our four children, Emma, Benjamin, Hannah-Marika and Jonathan who put up with my absences from them while I worked. They have always been fully supportive of all my work. My thanks, also, to Mrs Christine Watts, my secretary, whom I have never known to grumble despite the increasing demands from me on her time.

Last, but not least, I am grateful to God for saving me and calling me into this wonderful work of being an evangelist. May He, in all things, be glorified.

1 Where have all the evangelists gone?

In the horrors of the Second World War, the battle of El Alamein was a turning point. And yet, at one stage, victory for the allies would have seemed a mere dream. Throughout the summer of 1942 the Germans, under Rommel, were threatening Alexandria in Egypt. Its loss would have been devastating for the allies, and yet they did not have sufficient military power to prevent such an advance. What transformed the situation was the arrival and use of new American resources. These included a new design of tank which outclassed and outmanoeuvred the German military machine. These reinforcements brought about the most brilliant victory at El Alamein. Sir Winston Churchill said, 'Before Alamein we never had a victory, after Alamein we never had a defeat.'

In recent decades the Christian church in the West has seen serious losses. There does not appear to be that sharp, cutting edge in evangelistic work which makes the world sit up and take note of the claims of Christian truth. Are we perhaps needing additional resources? Or are we perhaps failing to use the resources and gifts which God has given for the Christian church? There is no easy panacea to reverse recent trends, but God has given evangelists to the church, and if we overlook his provision, can we realistically expect to make advances into enemy territory?

Lord Beaverbrook, the founder of the British newspaper, The *Daily Express*, wrote:

> The evangelist is the man who has the greatest capacity for doing good and therefore, if I were in a position to influence the life of a sincere young man today, I would say to him, 'Rather choose to be an evangelist than a cabinet minister or a millionaire.' When I was a young man I pitied my father for being a poor man and a preacher of the Word. Now that I am older, I envy him, his life and his career.

Billy Graham, speaking in 1986 at the Second International Congress for Itinerant Evangelists in Amsterdam, reckoned that worldwide there were nearly 50,000 evangelists. However, in the western world, evangelists appear to be a diminishing, and often disgraced, group of people. We have Christian dramatists, clowns, mime artists and magicians. We have godly pastors and Bible teachers, as well as singers whose ministry feeds the flock of God; but where have all the evangelists gone? Where are the people who are called by God to give their life to reaching the lost with the gospel?

A JOURNALIST'S VIEW

The church's apparent lack of concern or commitment to reach out to the lost world can be bewildering to the unsaved as well.

In 1994 Matthew Parris was made newspaper columnist of the year. He is a political sketch writer for *The Times*, an ex-Member of Parliament, sceptical about Christianity. Writing in *The Times*, he said:

> The New Testament offers a picture: a God who does not sound at all vague to me. He has sent His Son to Earth. He has distinct plans for each of us personally and can communicate directly with us. We are capable of forming a direct relationship, individually, with Him, and are commanded to try. We are told this can be done only through His Son. And we are offered the prospect of eternal life – an afterlife in happy, blissful or glorious circumstances – if we live this life in a certain manner.
>
> Friends, if I believed that, or even a tenth of that, how could I care which version of the prayer book was being used? I would drop my job, sell my house, throw away my possessions, leave my acquaintances and set out into the world burning with desire to know more and, when I had found out more, to act upon it and tell others.
>
> How is it possible to be indifferent to the possibility, if one believes it to be a possibility, that a being of this order makes demands of this order upon you or me, and that in 30, 20, 10 years – perhaps tomorrow – we shall be taken from this life and ushered into a new one whose nature will depend upon our obedience, now, to His will? Far from being puzzled that the Mormons or Adventists should knock on my door, I am unable to understand how anyone who believed that what is written in the Bible could choose to spend his waking hours in any other endeavour.

His explanation of the gospel may not be absolutely accurate, but the rebuke is an indictment on all Christians.

The popular caricature of the evangelist is of someone sweeping into town in a blaze of glory; extravagant dress, luxurious lifestyle, exaggerated claims and charismatic personality. Brash, belligerent, beguiling and boastful are the characteristics of the evangelist picked up and promoted by the media in films like *Elmer Gantry*, *Leap of Faith* or *The Apostle*. Theological liberals often find themselves in agreement with the media, simply using their images to bolster liberal attitudes and ideologies.

THE CHURCH AND THE EVANGELIST

Something of this has spilled over into the Christian church. After all, was it not evangelists who brought disgrace upon the church in the American 'Pearly-gate' scandals in the 1980s? It would seem natural, then, to eye with suspicion those who promote themselves and their ministry. The evangelist is often at the receiving end of veiled criticism from godly preachers who rightly are concerned for integrity in those who profess Christ. The itinerant lifestyle is seen as an easy escape from the responsibility of pastoral duties.

Frankly, sometimes even the more faithful evangelist appears to be a 'good communicator' but not a man of the Book. The method of evangelism – the programme, and the message – must commend the two pillars of the gospel: to repent and believe. A worldly programme undermines the very essence of what we want to communicate. The evangelist is often perceived as being a good salesperson, able to make an appeal, and stir people to commitment, *but to what*?

The church has raised other questions concerning the evangelist. Some would dispute whether the office of evangelist even exists today, arguing that all Christians should be evangelists to some extent. Others perceive the person working as an evangelist as starting on one of the lower rungs of the ladder of Christian service, but eventually being promoted to some other (higher) area of Christian ministry. This attitude is demonstrated by the oft-repeated question to evangelists, 'Do you think that one day you will become a pastor?' or by denominational groupings who will accredit pastors but not evangelists as 'ministers'. I am aware that the term 'evangelist' only occurs three times in Scripture; but then 'bishop' or 'elder', designating one who presides in the congregation, is used in only three passages, the word 'Christian' and the title 'deacon' in two verses of the Bible, and 'pastor' in only one. But as A. R. May says in *The New Testament Order for Church and Missionary*, 'There is ample evidence both in Scripture and the history of the early church to give us a clear understanding of the true significance of all five terms.'

'AN ENDANGERED SPECIES'

In his autobiography, *Be Myself*, Warren Wiersbe calls itinerant evangelists an 'endangered species'! Church-based evangelists also are few and far between. Though courses in 'evangelism' are readily accessible, who is specifically teaching and training evangelists? Sadly, many enthusiastic young people go to Bible College with a burden to preach the gospel to the unconverted and to win souls for Christ, only to discover that there is little emphasis on the practicalities of outreach, and even less on the work of the evangelist. All too often they find that they are being redirected into pastoral work or Bible teaching. We desperately need pastors and Bible teachers, and should praise God when such are being raised up. There must be evangelical truth for those who want to know (that is, believers), but we need *evangelistic truth* for those who do not want to know (that is, unbelievers). I am concerned that would-be evangelists are being redirected away from their natural gifting and calling. This leads to frustration in ministry in later years, and a loss for the body and cause of Christ today.

The growth of missionary endeavour over the last three centuries is something for which we praise God. There are many avenues of service for Christian people who are called to serve God in countries other than their homeland, but the work of the evangelist is vital. Pioneer workers, church planters and itinerant preachers on mission fields are, in reality, evangelists. One wonders if sometimes the only feasible way for someone to exercise their evangelistic gift, burden and calling is to serve as a missionary.

Another reason why evangelists are 'an endangered species' is that few evangelists remain at their work for more than a decade. There will always be an unevangelized world out there to be reached with the gospel, nevertheless there is a tendency (temptation?) to move to other ministries. Sometimes, of course, the move will be a genuine leading of the Lord; however, the pressure for results from an evangelist can be a wearing one, and may be a cause for some to consider other ministries. Also, evangelistic zeal is frequently perceived as a quality of the young. Thus, the calling of the evangelist is seen all too often as a young person's contribution to Christian work. Yet passion and fire should characterize all those walking closely with the Lord, and are not characteristics to be outgrown with the unfolding of a life. Young people need to be presented with the claims of Christ, but so does the older generation.

'To raise the dead'

The gifting of the evangelist is a unique one. Being an evangelist governs the way one presents evangelical truth. In the early part of the twentieth century, Samuel Chadwick founded Cliff College, a training college for Methodist evangelists. He testifies as to what marked out his ministry and gift:

> Before I entered the ministry, I was called upon to tackle a comparatively empty chapel. Hundreds of families in the district were

notoriously godless, and many of the men were of a desperate character. All methods were tried by us and without avail, and in our
despair we sought guidance and power in special prayer. A gracious work of sanctification began, old sins were confessed, and
old quarrels healed; and there came, as by inspiration, a prayer that
God would send us a Lazarus – a sinner so notorious, offensive
and hopeless, that the people would be compelled to see the power
of God. Our prayer was heard, 'Lazarus' came forth and took his
place among us, and from that hour the Church was crowded with
the neglected, despised and outcast. That settled my first working
principle. The way to fill a chapel is to raise the dead.

Every witness has a certain amount of authority, not least evangelists. They are ambassadors. They have the right to speak, for
this is God's earth, and they are proclaiming God's message.
Our authority comes from Christ who has called and commissioned us. It was He who said, 'All authority has been given to
me in heaven and on earth. Go therefore....' (Matt. 28:18-19).
Christians are to go in the Lord's name and make disciples of
all nations. We are not to be intimidated by others, but neither
are we to abuse the good name of the Lord Jesus whom we
represent. We 'go in' to know Christ and 'go out' to make him
known (John 10:9). Alexander Whyte worked in one church for
forty-seven years, first as an assistant pastor and then as the senior pastor. He always spent from 8 am to 2 pm with the Lord.
On one occasion after hearing his sermon, a member of the congregation said to him, 'You preached today as if you'd come
straight from the presence of Jesus.' Whyte replied, 'I did.'
Such communion with the Lord is the source of our authority.
The evangelist is the person whose gifting, calling and ministry
are devoted to proclaiming the good news single mindedly to
unconverted men and women.

MANY WORKS OF THE EVANGELIST

The evangelist, who is a herald of the gospel, will not necessarily be involved in mass-evangelism. Mass-evangelism is vital, and by no means a thing of the past. As Edward Murphy argued in *Christianity Today* (volume 19 issue 11), 1975), one cannot reject mass-evangelism without violating the Scripture, or deny its effectiveness without ignoring church history. It is particularly effective with those who have a more positive attitude toward the gospel, but are still unconverted. At least, the Word of God is being preached and the Holy Spirit uses His Word to glorify the Father through the Son.

However, many evangelists are involved in a less public but no less vital witness among the unsaved, that might be described as gleaning. In the book of Ruth (2:17) we read: 'So she gleaned in the field until evening, and beat out what she had gleaned, and it was about an ephah of barley.' Gleaning is a quaint illustration for those involved in personal work. Reaping on a larger scale has been done, but there are leftovers and corners which the reaper does not touch. The gleaner has to have eyes open for the opportunity. He or she has to bend for each piece which is picked up – one cannot glean with a stiff back. Gleaning is humble work, but each piece helps to make a bundle. The gleaner is as careful to retain as to obtain the harvest. Jean Francois Millet's famous painting of *The Gleaners* pictures what is involved. The gleaner pictures the personal work of the evangelist.

Evangelists reaching the masses will want to be involved in personal work as well. Such contact keeps evangelists from being puffed up and helps them to keep in touch with the people they will be preaching to. As a preacher, I find personal work vital for my ministry. It is not only an effective way of outreach, but it helps to remind me of where people are in their thinking concerning God. Evangelists will want to proclaim this gospel to their own friends, as well as to those people that other Christians have brought along. D. L. Moody, the evangelist, Dawson Trotman, founder of the Navigators, and many others have found it a good discipline to speak about the Lord to at least one unconverted person each day.

Personal work is vital and it can also be very precious to the heart of the preacher of the gospel. It does us good, as this story about a seventeenth-century Scottish preacher shows. James Guthrie had lost his way and decided that the best course of action was to let the reins of his horse rest on the saddle, and see where his horse would lead him. It took him to a little cottage. Knocking on the door, he found a Roman Catholic priest about to leave a dying woman and a grieving family. After the priest left, he asked whether the woman had received peace. She had not, so he explained the gospel to her and, before she died, she had believed and received the peace of God. Upon returning home, Guthrie said to his wife that he found the woman in a state of nature, led her to a state of grace, and left her in a state of glory!

CONCLUSION

It is time for the church to ask itself the straightforward question, 'Where and why have all the evangelists gone?' Are we trying to fight a war without the ammunition and armaments necessary for victory? Someone once said, 'We need men and women who have this balanced attitude and conviction – people who are humble before God, and are aware that their power comes from His indwelling Holy Spirit, but who are confirmed in their minds that God has given them a high calling as His ambassadors.'

'Now, Lord...grant to your servants that with all boldness they may speak your word' (Acts 4:29).

May we all echo in our hearts these words from *The Triumph of John and Betty Stam*:

> See, all the careless multitudes
> Are passing by, now passing by.
> The world is sick with sin and woe.
> All men must die, some day must die.
> The time set for our Lord's return
> Is drawing nigh, draws ever nigh.
> Send us in all Thy cleansing power –
> Lord, here am I! Here, Lord, am I!

2 God's agenda for each generation
Luke 24:44-49

Toward the end of his Gospel, Luke recalls 'the Great Commission' that Jesus gave to His disciples. Luke's focus is on the content of the message that we are to proclaim to our neighbours and the nations.

In Luke 24 we are told of Jesus' resurrection appearance to the two walking on the road to Emmaus. Jesus both *opened* the eyes of Cleopas and his friend and *opened* the Scriptures to them. Then to all His disciples, He *opened* their understanding so that they might comprehend the Scriptures. Speaking only days after His crucifixion, burial and resurrection (think about that!), He drove home the central, crucial core truths of the gospel:

- Christ had to suffer
- He rose from the dead

- Repentance and remission of sins should be proclaimed to all nations

- The Holy Spirit would empower them

In so speaking, He was giving us the mission of the church. We are to proclaim His death and resurrection urging people to repent so that they might receive forgiveness. Obedience to this is the only criteria as to whether we are being faithful to His heart's desire and agenda for the church. This, and this only, is the gospel.

This is relevant for those who call themselves 'apologists', who defend the faith, yet fail to explain the meaning of the cross and power of the resurrection. When Peter wrote urging that we 'give a reason for the hope that lies within us', surely *the* reason is that Jesus suffered and died, and that He rose and can forgive sin. I don't believe Peter is arguing that our proclamation is about quoting academics who spoke warmly of Christianity! Of course, evidence is crucial, and needs to be taught, but we should be determined to know nothing in our proclamation but Christ and Him crucified.

It is noble and good to give porridge to the poor, to save the whale, for street pastors to provide flip-flops for drunken revellers, to teach agriculture and provide irrigation systems for the developing world, to be environmentally friendly and serve the community. Such endeavours may even be used to build a bridge to people so that we can tell them about Jesus, but these are not what gospel ministry is about. Of course, kindness and good deeds will characterise the Christian. We want to do good – it comes naturally to the believer. But the great commission is to go and tell, to preach and proclaim, to warn and welcome sinners as we introduce them to Christ. Topping the agenda of church meetings ought always to be strategically reviewing and planning the programme of fulfilling Jesus' words before His ascension.

My daily newspaper recently reported that churches in the last year have provided 10 million 'man hours' to local authorities to help them in times of financial cuts. If local councils ask us to run youth clubs and care for the needy, praise God, but only if they are happy for us to present the gospel and speak about Jesus. I read recently, 'Sometimes people talk as if by renovating a city park or turning a housing slum into affordable, liveable apartments, we are extending God's reign over that park or that neighbourhood ... but the kingdom isn't geographical. Rather, it is defined relationally and dynamically; it exists where knees and hearts bow to the King and submit to Him ... Good deeds are good, but they don't broaden the kingdom of God.'[1] Eternal blessing, that which does extend the kingdom, only comes when sinners renounce sin and trust the crucified Christ as Lord and Saviour.

Jesus went through the villages and towns to preach. Moved with compassion He healed people there, but that was never His mission – His prime motivation – in going to these places. The Book of Acts tells the wonderful story of the gospel spreading from Jerusalem to Judea, then to Samaria and the uttermost parts of the earth. It does not speak of Christians working for the social betterment of Jerusalem and Antioch. Paul gave his life to the saving of the lost and the establishing of churches in good doctrine, so that they would continue the work of proclaiming the suffering, risen Jesus to people who would find forgiveness if they repented. Our mission is to proclaim what Jesus has accomplished.

---

1   Taken from, *What is the mission of the church?* by Kevin DeYoung & Greg Gilbert, (Crossway: Chicago, 2011).

The greatest act of friendship that we can show anyone is to introduce them to Jesus. The greatest act of tyranny is to ignore a person's plight and not warn them of their desperate need to repent and find forgiveness from God.

Luke 24:49 is thoroughly Trinitarian: the Promise of the Father, the plan of the Son, the power of the Spirit. God's power is promised as we proclaim the suffering Saviour. We must explain the hidden work of Christ as He bore our sin in His own body on the cross. Our rebellion was laid on Jesus so that we might be forgiven and have His righteousness laid on us. We are to make known that Jesus is risen. The hearers' part is to repent, and God's response is to give forgiveness of sin. What a message! There is nothing here to be ashamed about, nothing to brush under the carpet, nothing for which we should be embarrassed. It is the most glorious theme. Do we know of anything or anyone who is more worthy of being spoken about than Jesus? Is any remedy effective in dealing with people's sins and self-destruction other than Jesus? Isn't the greatest demonstration of love to others is to tell them of God's demonstration of love towards us? Who has the right to intimidate us into silence about the gospel? We dare not be sidetracked from proclaiming Christ and Him crucified in our pulpits, to our friends or in our strategy of Christian work. Who has told preachers that they need to be positive-thinking, feel-good preachers, when people around them are perishing? The missionary hymn says it so well: 'Every person in every nation, in each succeeding generation, has the right to hear the news that Christ can save.' This is the mission of the church.

3 Old Testament 'evangelists'

Fashionable new ideas about *the way* to do God's work in the current culture burst on to the Christian scene at frequent intervals. Seminars and conferences are taken on their rounds, and they have their influence. A work which has been particularly blessed of the Lord becomes a prototype for others. Some of these make a valid contribution to the task of evangelism, though one cannot franchise the work of God.

GOD USES INDIVIDUALS

God's underlying method, however, has always been to take individuals and use them. God chose Joseph to deliver Egypt and His people from starvation; Moses to lead them out of slavery; Joshua to lead them into the promised land; the judges were raised up personally by God, as were the prophets. The list of such characters in Scripture is long and impressive, but why did God choose these people?

God looks for individuals to 'stand in the gap' (Ezek. 22:30). All God's gracious dealings prepared them for their distinctive roles, nevertheless God is looking for qualities which He can use. David is an obvious example here. He is marked out as an individual who had both integrity and skill and is described as 'a man after [God's] own heart' (Acts 13:22). Undoubtedly, God blesses particular organizations and churches, but His method is to take, fill and use individuals committed to Him.

Such individuals are not mavericks, speaking whatever thoughts they dream up. Jeremiah 23:9-40 clearly exposes such people. But the person who seeks to honour the Lord will always proclaim the Word of God. God uses the people who proclaim the Word, which God is committed to use! Jeremiah testified to this, saying:

> Your words were found, and I ate them, and Your word was to me
> the joy and rejoicing of my heart; for I am called by your name,
> O LORD God of hosts. (Jer. 15:16)

and 'Is not My word like a fire?' says the LORD, 'And like a hammer that breaks the rock in pieces?' (Jer. 23:29). There is a fire in the heart of the true evangelist, which leads to a desire for complete commitment to proclaiming the Word, to fulfil the calling from the Lord.

PREACHERS OF THE WORD

Albert Knudson said: 'There are two classes of preachers: the good preachers who have something to say and the poor preachers who have to say something. But there is yet another and higher class. It consists of those who have something to say and have to say it. Such are the prophets.' Throughout the unfolding drama of the Bible, God liberally scatters biographies – some thumbnail sketches; others, full, detailed life-stories – of preachers of the Word. They hold a special place in God's heart. The world needs the Word. These Old Testament prophets were real evangelists not only because they preached the Word, but because they pointed people to Christ: 'These things Isaiah said when he saw His glory and spoke of Him' (John 12:41). The evangelist, the prophet and the exhorter each have the same spirit. God's people have the responsibility for bringing the Word of God to men and women in each succeeding generation.

In the opening chapters of the Bible, even before the time of the flood, we find God taking three people, and using them as preachers of the Word. Take Abel, for example. He and his brother Cain had the same parents, environment, and economic situation and were both devout; but one became a murderer, the other a martyr. Cain talked with Abel immediately prior to murdering him (Gen. 4:8), but his words were not conveyors of truth. It was Abel's faith, offering and blood which gave such an eloquent, yet disturbing message: they 'cried out' from the very ground where he lay (Gen. 4:10).

Then there was Enoch, described as one who 'walked with God', but in the New Testament, he is noted as one who preached, warning the people of impending judgment (Jude 14 and 15). He was 'the seventh from Adam', but still we see how God, in the early stages of human history, took a man and set the pattern: preaching the Word is to be His means of reaching out to needy people.

Finally and unforgettably, Noah built an ark. But as he laboured, he preached. Results were negligible – after 120 years of building and preaching only eight people were saved. In obeying God, Noah found loneliness, scorn, opposition, derision and ... 'grace in the eyes of the LORD' (Gen. 6:8).

These three great, early characters of world history all 'preached': Abel emphasized redemption through the blood, Enoch pleaded concerning judgment and the second coming of Christ, and Noah, by word and action, declared justification by faith. The people of their day had no excuse. They had heard the Word.

CONFRONTING THE PEOPLE

Throughout the rest of the Old Testament, God raised up such people. Prophets were called and commissioned, not necessarily to see great 'fruit' from their work, but at least to confront nations and populations with the Word of God. High on the Lord's agenda was the desire to spread His Word to all peoples. They were living in pre-Christ days. They preached forgiveness and restoration, and could do so because in the fullness of time Christ would come and die for sin. They preached a coming Saviour, but they were the true evangelists of their day, heralding the Word of God to those who were not walking with the Lord.

Centuries later, out of nowhere, came 'the father of the prophets' – Elijah. This trailblazer confronted a godless king and his nation with the Word of God. Later, Elisha was called to be a friend, helper and successor to Elijah. Having a double-portion of the spirit of his mentor, he too did battle with those who had been subtly entangled by the world, the flesh and the devil, and had turned their backs on the true and living God. Elijah and Elisha were men of courage who acted on orders given by their God, fearlessly preaching the Word and turning the hearts of many to righteousness.

It has been said that there are four steps to disaster and the destruction of a nation. First, there is a disregard for God, then disobedience to God, next a denial of God, and finally a defiance of God. It was in such a situation of rapid spiritual declension and impending judgement, that the word of the Lord came to young Jeremiah saying:

> Before I formed you in the womb I knew you; before you were born I sanctified you; *and* I ordained you a prophet to the nations. ...Behold I have put My words in your mouth. See, I have this day set you over the nations and over the kingdoms, to root out and to pull down, to destroy and to throw down, to build and to plant (Jer. 1:5 and 9-10).

Despite Jeremiah's objections concerning his youth and lack of eloquence, God promised his presence and gave his authority to Jeremiah, who would receive grace to fulfil the unenviable duty of rebuking the sins of the surrounding heathen nations, as well as those of God's people. Jeremiah's experience so drained him that he wrestled with the possibility of quitting and starting a motel:

> Oh, that I had in the wilderness a lodging place for wayfaring men; that I might leave my people and go from them! For they are all adulterers, an assembly of treacherous men. (Jer. 9:2)

But this could be only a passing thought. Jeremiah's calling was too sure and solid to be dislodged by his crosscurrents of emotions. He reasoned against, and answered his own temptations:

> O my soul, my soul! I am pained in my very heart!... I cannot hold my peace, because you have heard, O my soul, the sound of the trumpet, the alarm of war. (Jer. 4:19)

Later he also said:

> But *His* word was in my heart like a burning fire shut up in my bones; I was weary of holding it back, and I could not. (Jer. 20:9)

Preaching and the ministry were not just a career for Jeremiah: they cost him everything – the possibility of marriage, the natural desire for a quiet, comfortable existence, and possibly even his life. He suffered opposition, depression, rejection, strife, imprisonment, and oppression of the mind as he condemned idolatry, immorality, backsliding, false prophecy and compromise. Broken, he felt deeply the message which was on his heart and lips:

> Oh, that my head were waters, and my eyes a fountain of tears, that I might weep day and night for the slain of the daughter of my people! (Jer. 9:1)

Jeremiah prayed, preached, wrote books and letters, and trained others so that the Word of God might be made known to people around him. Above all else, he was faithful to the God he worshipped, who loved him faithfully with an everlasting love.

COSTLY OBEDIENCE

Ezekiel's commission was equally demanding. As a young man, he had been taken captive and was living in Babylon. Ezekiel was a priest, but God called him for something more. He was among the captives by the River Chebar, when (to quote from his testimony):

> ... the heavens were opened and I saw visions of God.... So when I saw it, I fell on my face, and I heard a voice of One speaking. And He said to me, "Son of man, stand on your feet, and I will speak to you." Then the Spirit entered me when He spoke to me, and set me on my feet; and I heard him who spoke to me. And He said to me, "Son of man, I am sending you to the children of Israel, to a rebellious nation that has rebelled against Me.... You shall speak My words to them, whether they hear or whether they refuse". ' (Ezek. 1:1, 28; 2:1-3, 7)

In obeying all that God had commanded him (on 49 occasions Ezekiel says, 'The Word of the LORD came to me'), Ezekiel spoke to the people, prophets, priests, princes, the elders and shepherds. He had a difficult message for difficult people. He spoke to the land of Israel and the city of Jerusalem, to leading heathen nations and even to inanimate objects such as dry bones, the wind, fowls, beasts and forests. He used symbols, visions, parables, poems, proverbs and prophecies in his communication. He was willing to lie in any position which God commanded him, to go into the plain, to shut himself up in the house, sacrifice his personal appearance, eat food by weight, move at a day's notice, and not to weep at the death of his wife even though he would weep bitterly for the sins of his people. For Ezekiel, personal duty to God was the overwhelming priority of his life.

In contrast, the prophet Jonah was going to witness possibly the greatest revival of all time. Nevertheless, he initially fled from the responsibility, having no love for the people he was called to warn. Amy Carmichael wrote some potent lines which, had they been penned in Jonah's day, might have caused him to think differently about his trip to Tarshish:

> Thou hast enough to pay thy fare?
> Well, be it so; but thou shouldst ask
> Did thy God send thee there?
> There's many a coin flung lightly down
> Brings back a load of care.
> It may cost what thou knowest not
> To bring thee back from there.

Jonah's reluctance to preach to the people of Nineveh is well known. And I suspect compassion did not characterize his sermon. All we have of his preaching is found in Jonah 3:4: 'Yet forty days, and Nineveh will be overthrown!' It was the king of Nineveh that spread the Word he had heard from Jonah (3:6-9). The vast city of Nineveh repented and Jonah became a most strangely disappointed evangelist. He had experienced God's grace and mercy, but selfishly did not want the Ninevites to share in the love of God. God overruled and mightily blessed his word. The book of Jonah teaches the importance of obedience to God's calling and the need for compassion for the lost. Where our love is inadequate, God's love and constraining will graciously overrule. He loves the lost world, and the wayward worker!

Ezra, on the other hand, is a fine example of a man using the Word of God to bring back the wayward people of God, to the ways of God: 'For Ezra had prepared his heart to seek the Law of the LORD, and to do it, and to teach statutes and ordinances in Israel' (Ezra 7:10). The results of this were outstanding: 'Then everyone who trembled at the words of the God of Israel assembled to me, because of the transgression of those who had been carried away captive, and I sat astonished until the evening sacrifice' (Ezra 9:4).

Each of the men that God used acted in obedience to the Lord. They were people of natural passions, who struggled with human frailties as any others would, but they had been gripped by a greater power and passion than their own. Something burned within them, so that they could not keep silent. They were convinced that there were lost, or at least backslidden people, who had to hear the Word of the Lord. God had commissioned them and they had no alternative but to go and proclaim what God had spoken to them. Anything less would have been an act of blatant disobedience, comparable only to the sins of the people they were supposed to be reaching.

Their message was not the gospel of the Lord Jesus Christ as we know it today for Christ was still to come. They proclaimed the Word of God, rebuking sin and speaking of forgiveness. The twin themes of the wrath of God and the grace of God combined to ensure that the Lord was heard and that the people were without excuse. God's word to Ezekiel (33:11) seems to summarize their message: ' "As I live," says the Lord GOD, "I have no pleasure in the death of the wicked, but that the wicked turn from his way and live. Turn, turn from your evil ways! For why should you die, O house of Israel?" '

These proclaimers of God's Word were like watchmen, and even though their message was not always obeyed, at least they did not have the blood of the people on their hands. Repentance and faith towards God is not a very popular message, in any generation.

UNSUNG HEROES

Not every Old Testament preacher has left his name as a permanent part of spiritual history. There are many unsung heroes who are known in heaven and were significant upon earth as they made known the Word of God. For example, in the days of King Jehoshaphat, we read that he appointed Levites who 'taught in Judah, and had the Book of the Law of the LORD with them; they went throughout all the cities of Judah and taught the people' (2 Chron. 17:9).

However, though we read that 'time would fail me to tell of others' (speaking of the prophets), God gave His abiding epitaph in Hebrews 11:

> The prophets: who through faith subdued kingdoms, worked righteousness, obtained promises, stopped the mouths of lions, quenched the violence of fire, escaped the edge of the sword, out of weakness were made strong, became valiant in battle, turned to flight the armies of the aliens. Women received their dead raised to life again. And others were tortured, not accepting deliverance, that they might obtain a better resurrection. Still others had trial of

mockings and scourgings, yes, and of chains and imprisonment. They were stoned, they were sawn in two, were tempted, were slain with the sword. They wandered about in sheepskins and goat-skins, being destitute, afflicted, tormented – of whom the world was not worthy. They wandered in deserts and mountains, in dens and caves of the earth. And all these... obtained a good testimony through faith ... (Heb. 11:32-39).

Before leaving the Old Testament, it is worth noting that many of these heroes of truth had the foresight and vision to invest and impart their burden to a succeeding generation. We read that David served his own generation, but it was in the heart of some to strive to serve future generations too. To that end they trained up younger men to take over from them. The Lord sent Samuel to be trained under Eli, Moses had his Joshua, Elijah his Elisha, and Jeremiah his Baruch. The heart of God appears to have become something of the heart of these men. There is a lesson here, which we will do well not to forget in our day.

4 Christ, the Evangelist

God yearns with all his heart for men and women to repent and believe. At the very beginning of time, God took the initiative and came looking for man, 'Then the LORD God called to Adam and said to him, "Where are you?" ' (Gen. 3:9), words that I believe were asked with tenderness and compassion. Afterwards, God immediately promised to the newly created, now fallen world that in the fullness of time, the Seed of a woman would bruise the head of the serpent (Gen. 3:15). True to his Word, 'The Father has sent the Son as Saviour of the world' (1 John 4:14).

Christ came not so much to preach the gospel, but that there might be a gospel to preach! When Christ had finished His work, there was nothing left for anyone else to do to gain salvation. Nevertheless, God's only begotten Son was a preacher. He spoke as no other man spoke. Unlike the religious leaders of His day,

His preaching was with authority. However, He was not only preaching with words but also with action; the two were utterly consistent. There was no duplicity in the person of Christ. When, at the age of thirty, Christ preached the Sermon on the Mount, he was only saying what he had been living for the past thirty years.

Lehman Strauss in his book, *The Godhead*, says:

> The primary purpose of Christ's coming into the world was to win the lost to personal faith in Himself as the Son of God and the Saviour of men. At no time did He allow other tasks, no matter how important they appeared to be, to relegate His primary purpose to the background. At times He engaged Himself in deeds of social service or, as in many instances, He spent time in training His disciples for service; but every task to which our Lord gave Himself had as its ultimate goal the salvation of the lost. This was the will of the Father, and to that end Jesus consecrated all His efforts, even to the sacrificing of His very life on the cross.

THE SENSE OF 'CALL'

Jesus was absolutely sure of His calling (see Luke 4:16-21, 43 and 19:10). He had been born that He might die and take on Himself the sins that cut us off from God and bring condemnation. One of His favourite words was 'sent', for He knew why He had come to this earth (John 20:21). James Stalker in *Christ Our Example* says:

> All the prophets and apostles who have dealt with men for God have been driven by this impulse [a sense of divine call], which has recovered them in hours of weakness and enabled them to face the opposition of the world. Most of them have experienced a crisis in which this call has come and clearly determined their lifework. It came to Moses in the wilderness and drove him into public life in spite of strong resistance...it came to Isaiah in a vision which coloured all his after history; and it revolutionised St. Paul's life in an hour. Jeremiah felt the divine message like a sword in his bones

and like a fire which consumed him.... This was one of the strongest motives of Christ's life also. It gave to it its irresistible momentum; it strengthened Him in the face of opposition; it rescued Him from the dark hour of despair.... His comfort was that every step He took was in fulfilment of the divine will.

OUR DIVINE EXAMPLE

Christ acted as an evangelist. James Stalker again expresses this well:

> 'The passing of Jesus throughout the country was like the passing of a magnet over a floor where there are pieces of iron: it drew the souls which had affinity for the divine life to itself .... He followed people to their earthly haunts, and so may we; but He followed them further – down to the gates of hell, where He plucked the prey from the hands of the mighty.'

Whereas the evangelists of today point people away from themselves to the Lord Jesus, Christ, as the Friend of sinners and the Saviour of the world, invited people to come to Him (Matt. 11:28-29). He said of Himself that He had come 'to seek and to save that which was lost' (Luke 19:10). He alone could give forgiveness and rest to the soul (Mark 2:7b). He is the wonderful Counsellor.

He is the pattern for all soul winning work. How tenderly he dealt with Zacchaeus, and the woman caught in the act of adultery, and the Samaritan woman. He started where people were, and He listened to what they were saying (see, for example, the way the conversation proceeded on the road to Emmaus in Luke 24:13-27). No doubt learning from this, Francis Schaeffer said that if he had thirty minutes with a non-Christian, he would listen for twenty-five and then speak. Jesus took people's questions seriously, as shown in the depth of the answers He gave (for example, Luke 10:25-37). He Himself used questions; He asked favours to start spiritual conversation, as with Zacchaeus or the Samaritan woman. But He did not force Himself on people. Compassion ruled all that He did. He had pity on the crowds who were like sheep without a shepherd and He prayed for forgiveness for the Roman soldiers who were crucifying Him (Matt. 9:36; Luke 23:34).

In talking with people, He always went to the heart of the problem, which, of course, is sin. He was slow to condemn sinners, but would not condone sin (see, for example, the accounts given in two of the Gospels of His dealings with sinners: Luke 7:36-50; John 5:1-18; 8:1-11).

Jesus called people out of their sin to repentance and faith, to new life in Him (John 10:10b). The common people heard Him gladly (Mark 12:37b). He mixed with and had a message for all: the waifs and strays of society, the unloved and unlovely, the outcasts and underdogs, as well as the respected well-to-do and religious leaders. Christ cared for and could cope with every need of the whole person. He healed the sick, cast out demons, restored children to their parents, and met each physical want. Christ always had the right word for each occasion and individual. There was no glib repetition of favourite phrases. In seeking always to glorify His Father, He constantly pointed men and women away from their sin to a new life, lived in the power of God and for the glory of God. He was able and willing to forgive sins, and at the climax of His life, He died bearing in His body the sin of the world.

Prayer was at the heart of all that the Lord Jesus did. His dependency on prayer is seen in many places in the Gospels. For example, 'having risen a long while before daylight, He went out and departed to a solitary place; and there He prayed' (Mark 1:35); 'But when He saw the multitudes, He was moved with compassion for them, because they were weary and scattered, like sheep having no shepherd. Then He said to His disciples, "The harvest truly is plentiful, but the labourers are few. Therefore pray the Lord of the harvest to send out labourers into His harvest" ' (Matt. 9:36-38).

To be with Christ, as were His twelve chosen disciples, was to be in the centre of evangelistic action. Where He was, God was. Where He was working, God was working. For those who met or heard Him, He was either a savour of life or a savour of death. He was constantly seeking people, and He gave himself completely to the people who sought Him. Nobody was the same after being confronted with Christ. Neutrality was banished once one had met Him. He was unforgettable. He has, throughout time, been the focal point of world history.

CHRIST'S COMMAND

Having been the supreme example of a soul winner, Christ then commanded His followers to proclaim the gospel. Christlike Christians will seek to speak to those they meet, introducing them to the Lord Jesus Christ. This is not always easy work, as Paul made clear when he addressed the believers in Galatia as 'My little children, for whom I labour in birth again until Christ is formed in you' (Gal. 4:19). We will find that we too must 'bleed' if we would bless. As the Scripture closes, we find again the loving Lord Jesus making His final plea as an evangelist to all who are thirsty, 'And the Spirit and bride say, "Come!" And let him who hears say, "Come!" And let him who thirsts come. And whoever desires, let him take the water of life freely' (Rev. 22:17).

This verse in Revelation also expresses Christ's desire that those who 'hear' should be saying to others, 'Come!' The work of making known the gospel to a lost world was the final heartfelt instruction given by Christ, on earth, to His followers. As He commanded, He promised His presence: 'Go...and lo I am with you.' That in itself is sufficient encouragement to obey.

In one sense, all Christians are to be evangelists. The apostle Paul reminded timid Timothy, pastoring a church, that he, too, was to fulfil his ministry and 'do the work of an evangelist' (2 Tim. 4:5). However, there are those who are not just under the general command, given to all believers, to evangelize, but who are specially gifted, equipped, skilled and called to be evangelists. God 'Himself gave some to be apostles, some prophets, some evangelists, and some pastors and teachers, for the equipping of the saints for the work of ministry, for the edifying of the body of Christ' (Eph. 4:11-12).

This verse from Ephesians 4 is a key verse. The apostles and prophets referred to are the establishers of the faith. The pastors and teachers are the edifiers of the flock; but the evangelists are the extenders of the frontiers. In Ephesians 2:19-22 we read that the apostles and prophets were foundational, so that they come to us today through the Scriptures, but there is no suggestion that the evangelist is foundational only. It is a gift, given by the Lord himself, to the church, to be used in reaching out to the unconverted that they may hear the gospel and believe in the Lord Jesus and be saved, to the glory of God.

To neglect this gift is effrontery to the Lord himself. It is an undermining of the example established by the Lord Jesus, and a thwarting of the preparations of God in the life of some Christians. 'For we are his workmanship, created in Christ Jesus for good works, which God prepared beforehand that we should walk in them' (Eph. 2:10). It is a restricting of the means God ordained for the widespread heralding of the good news of Jesus Christ. As Christians and churches who are serious in our desire to live for Christ in our day, we need to examine ourselves, as well as our strategy of evangelization. We should seek to bring all our attitudes and actions into line with the biblical pattern for evangelism.

5 The Holy Spirit as an Evangelist

Imagine a convention of blind men healed by Jesus. They have met together to discuss the nature of their experience. They are all grateful for what the Lord Jesus has done for them, but the question is: What is the 'definitive experience'? Is it the Word of Jesus? Or is it His touch or spitting upon their eyes? Is there to be one touch or two? Do I have to throw away my cloak? Is mud necessary? (See Matt. 9:27-29; 20:29-34; Mark 8:22-26; 10:46-52; Luke 18:35-42; John 9:1-7).

There is obviously a common factor – all were truly healed, but they would not be able to stereotype their experiences. Hopefully the blind men now healed would have something more useful to discuss!

When we look at Christian conversion and the work of the Holy Spirit there is a similar variety of experience. What a contrast between Lydia, 'whose heart the Lord opened', and the jailer who needed an earthquake before he asked the way of salvation. The common factor was that the Holy Spirit used the Word of God (Acts 16:14, 30-32). God deals with people as individuals, even if they are in a crowd. It follows, therefore, that there will be a variety of religious experiences, but the Holy Spirit will be at work in each person, and He will use His Word.

THE CONVICTING WORK OF THE HOLY SPIRIT

Jesus spoke most fully about the Holy Spirit's work in both the unbelieving world and the believer in John 16:4-15. To the unbeliever, in the world, the Holy Spirit convicts of sin. Jesus said, 'And when He has come, He will convict the world of sin, and of righteousness, and of judgment' (John 16:8). He brings home certain truths to the mind and the conscience. Imagine that you are driving your car when you see in your mirror the flashing light of a police car. Suddenly, a thousand and one questions flash through your mind: 'Was I speeding? Did I indicate to turn? Is my insurance up to date?...' When the Holy Spirit is working in a person's mind, he or she begins to consider past sins, recognizing faults and failures in the sight of God. The Holy Spirit '[convicts] of sin, because they do not believe in Me...' (16:9). Of course, sin is the ultimate problem of human beings who are separated from the God who made us to enjoy a relationship with himself. In Mark 7:21-23, Jesus taught that our sinful actions come from a sinful heart. We are in spiritual darkness (Acts 26:18 and Col. 1:13), spiritually dead (Eph. 2:1), and guilty of having a hostile mind and doing evil deeds (Col. 1:21). The Holy Spirit impresses this true state of people upon individuals. For example, Paul felt he was fulfilling the law of God (Phil. 3:6), until the Holy Spirit using the Word showed him his true spiritual state.

The Holy Spirit convicts of righteousness, which is the righteousness of Christ, contrasted with our lack of it. He alone was holy from birth (Luke 1:35) and fulfilled all the demands of God. His obedience was unto death. (Phil. 2:8). He was able to say that He had always done that which pleases the Father (John 8:29). On the cross He offered to God the one perfect sacrifice for sin, discharging the sinner's debt by bearing the punishment which was our due (Rom. 3:24-25; 2 Cor. 5:21; 1 Pet. 2:24; 3:18). The Holy Spirit bears witness to this, which was the Father's purpose in sending His Son (Gal. 4:4-6). Christ's obedience was perfect and His sacrifice complete (Heb. 10:12-14), and through it the Holy Spirit can create faith which brings about salvation. Through faith we are covered with the perfect righteousness of Christ.

The Holy Spirit also convicts of judgment to come. The Lord Jesus has already judged Satan at the cross: 'the ruler of this world is judged' (John 16:11; also John 12:31; Col. 2:14-15). If the leader has been judged, what hope is there for his followers? In Matthew 12:29, Jesus had spoken of the binding of the 'strong man', so that captives could be released. The cross was the place where this was completed. Satan is condemned to lose his power, and salvation is proclaimed.

The Holy Spirit shows people their need of a Saviour and how the Lord Jesus Christ, God's provision, meets this need. It is the Holy Spirit who brings about new birth. In John 3:5, speaking of the new birth, Jesus speaks of being born of the Spirit. Interestingly, in 1 Peter 1:23 we read about being born anew by the incorruptible seed of the Word of God. The lesson is that the Spirit and the Word work together, and bring about new birth. We see this illustrated in Ezekiel's vision of dry bones where the wind of the Spirit and the Word of God brought life out of death. It is a common temptation to look despairingly at certain individuals and feel that there is no hope of them ever being converted. 'Can these dry bones live?' – we feel the tone of desperation in our hearts. But, as the Word is proclaimed, the Holy Spirit takes it, and works in such a way as to bring about a movement, a rattling, a noise, and bone is joined to bone to form first the skeleton, then the corpse; and as breath comes, real life. What happened in Ezekiel's vision (see Ezekiel 37), happens so often in the lives of men and women. Dry, dead bones can come to life as the Spirit and the Word work together in individuals.

The Holy Spirit comes to live within the new convert. Conversion is described in these terms: 'Then Peter said to them, "Repent, and let every one of you be baptized in the name of Jesus Christ for the remission of sins; and you shall receive the gift of the Holy Spirit"' (Acts 2:38). It is the sincere desire of the Holy Spirit, with the Lord Jesus Himself, that men and women should come to know the true and living God, and find in Him their satisfaction. 'And the Spirit and the bride say, "Come!" And let him who hears say, "Come!" And let him who thirsts come. And whoever desires, let him take the water of life freely' (Rev. 22:17). Notice in this verse, God is acting as an evangelist, as the Holy Spirit urges people to 'Come!', then He pleads with the hearers to be evangelists, and finally God speaks as the Evangelist again. No human evangelist can better this earnest pleading which expresses the tender heart of God. The Holy Spirit convicts, convinces and converts.

PRAYING EARNESTLY

All work of proclaiming the gospel is to be done in dependence upon God. As we preach Jesus, we will pray for the Holy Spirit to take hold of the holy Word of God and apply it to the unholy hearts of men and women, transforming them into people who, above all else, desire Him who is holy. The devotional life of the evangelist is to be exercised daily in order to be kept strong. If we are to see great blessing and people coming to faith in Christ, there must be a work of God. The evangelist will pray that the Lord would accomplish that which is impossible for the evangelist to achieve in his own strength, namely, the saving of souls.

Colossians 4:2 is translated in a variety of ways, but all have in common a sense of the extreme importance of prayer: 'Continue earnestly in prayer' (NKJV), or 'Devote yourselves to prayer' (NIV and New Living Translation), or 'Pray diligently' (The Message), or 'Always maintain the habit of prayer' (Phillips). Similar encouragements to pray are found in Romans 12:12, Ephesians 6:18 and 1 Thessalonians 5:17. When Paul was in prison, instead of praying for an open prison door, he prayed for a door of opportunity to be opened to him (Col. 4:3). He knew that only the Holy Spirit could give a great and effective opening (1 Cor. 16:9). Even though the evangelist may be busy there is no excuse for starving, stinting or scurrying prayer. Paul prayed (and fasted) for himself, for those possessed by Satan, when in pain or song, with friends and for friends, for the sick, for lost souls, for the believers' spiritual warfare, edification, power, fellowship, guidance and work, as well as for individual believers.

Paul was following the example of the Lord Jesus who prayed incessantly and set a standard that no evangelist would dare ignore. If Christ prayed, it would be supreme arrogance to think we need not, yet one fears that prayerlessness (practical atheism) is a common blight of many would-be evangelists.

Evangelism is supremely the work of the Holy Spirit, and therefore time for seeking His blessing is very much a part of the overall work of evangelism. It is He who gives strength to the evangelist to do the work, which at times is spiritually, emotionally and physically exhausting. Many a time I have inwardly prayed for 'resurrection power' to keep going in witnessing or preaching, because I have felt exhausted. The Holy Spirit uses the gifts and skills that are ours to make them count for eternity. Human skills, strength and stamina are insufficient to bring men and women to Christ. Our sufficiency is of Christ. The Holy Spirit enables, equips, energizes and empowers that we might be effective in the work of evangelism.

The Manila Manifesto, produced during the Second International Congress on World Evangelisation in 1989, included this paragraph headed 'God the Evangelist':

> The Scriptures declare that God himself is the chief evangelist. For the Spirit of God is the Spirit of truth, love, holiness and power, and evangelism is impossible without him. It is he who anoints the messenger, confirms the word, prepares the hearer, convinces the sinful, enlightens the blind, gives life to the dead, enables us to repent and believe, unites us to the body of Christ, assures us that we are God's children, leads us into Christ-like character and service, and sends us out in our turn to be Christ's witnesses. In all this the Holy Spirit's main preoccupation is to glorify Jesus Christ by showing him to us and forming him in us.

6 New Testament evangelists

There is a note of irony in Luke 3:1-2: 'Now in the fifteenth year of the reign of Tiberius Caesar, Pontius Pilate being governor of Judea, Herod being tetrarch of Galilee, his brother Philip tetrarch of Iturea and the region of Trachonitus, and Lysanias tetrarch of Abilene, Annas and Caiaphas being high priests, the word of God came to John the son of Zacharias in the wilderness.' Seven political and religious leaders are listed, but the word of God came to John in the wilderness! He was not ashamed to repeat his message: 'Behold the Lamb of God' (John 1:29, 36), for Christ crucified was John's theme. We know John was effective in his preaching for we read: 'Then many came to Him [Jesus] and said, "John performed no sign, but all the things that John spoke about this Man were true." And many believed in Him there' (John 10:41-42). John the Baptist's disciples, Andrew and John, were so convinced by his message that they left him to follow Jesus Christ. John the Baptist was bold and very pointed as he rooted out sin, clearly explaining the nitty-gritty implications of repentance.

Jesus' disciples' first 'evangelistic' endeavours are described in the Gospels. The disciples had been in Christ's company, had witnessed His miracles, heard His teaching, learned how to pray and live, and now were sent forth to evangelize their country-men. The purpose was twofold: to teach the disciples, and to meet the spiritual needs of the people. They were, after all, like sheep without a shepherd and Christ wanted them to know of His love for them.

Their work was in the province of Galilee. It made quite an impact, even attracting the attention of the king (Mark 6:14). A. B. Bruce in his classic book *The Training of the Twelve* says:

> The area was limited, to build a strong and secure base to begin with, and perhaps their hearts were too narrow, their prejudices too strong; there was too much Jew and too little Christian in their thinking at this time. If they had gone in to a Samaritan area, there could have been political or religious disputes.

It seems that the miraculous works were great, but preaching was quite limited. At this time, of course, their knowledge was very basic, though they were aware of the importance of repentance if people were to enter the kingdom of heaven.

THE SEVENTY

Herod heard of their work, however, and great crowds appear to have accompanied the disciples as they moved from place to place. It is unlikely that there was much lasting spiritual impact made at this time, but it was a beginning. Later Jesus appointed seventy to accompany the disciples. Jesus' reference to the 'wise and prudent' implies that it was ordinary folk who believed.

The evangelistic tour was successful, but the Lord warned against pride and elation (Luke 10:20). Fruitfulness does not necessarily mean godliness (Matt. 7:22). Soon afterwards Christ said, 'Come aside by yourselves...and rest awhile' (Mark 6:31), and in so doing he showed this perfect understanding of the needs of the twelve – caring for their minds and their jaded bodies.

The twelve were told to rely entirely on the providence of God. It was natural for the disciples to be fearful, especially after John the Baptist's recent beheading because he had preached repentance. But Jesus taught the disciples that God would provide all that they needed. He assumed that in each city there would be at least one worthy person. But He did warn them that things would not be easy for them. Amidst all the dangers there should be caution and faithfulness. In warning them to 'beware of men', He was saying that they should not be so simple as to imagine that all people are honest, good, fair and tolerant. They were to remember that there are wolves in the world.

Christ taught that the souls of all are precious, but that if one city does not receive the message and the messenger, they should move on to the next. As A. B. Bruce puts it, 'The disciples were in peril of trial, mockery, violence and even of their own lives. Jesus reminds His disciples that there are two types of death – with the sword, and through unfaithfulness to duty.'

THE EVERYDAY WITNESS

After the death and rising again of Jesus, the book of Acts contains three snapshots of evangelism. First, there is the picture of the witness: 'But you shall receive power when the Holy Spirit has come upon you, and you shall be witnesses to Me in Jerusalem, and in all Judea and Samaria, and to the end of the earth' (Acts 1:8). The word 'witness' is used twenty-nine times in the New Testament. There were to be ever-extending concentric circles of witness; first in Jerusalem, then Judea, then Samaria, and eventually the uttermost parts of the earth. The early church took Christ's commission seriously: 'And daily in the temple, and in every house, they did not cease teaching and preaching Jesus as the Christ' (Acts 5:42). Six times in the book of Acts there is a progress report on the effectiveness of their evangelism (6:7; 9:31; 12:24; 16:5; 19:20; 28:31).

There is even an anonymous witness/evangelist referred to in 2 Corinthians 8:18: 'And we have sent with him the brother whose praise is in the gospel throughout all the churches.' Some commentators have wondered if this is Luke. It seems that Luke felt at ease travelling, and here whoever is being written about had earned the commendation of the churches for being a gospel person.

Those first Christians were like the early Methodists to whom it was said, 'You have nothing to do but to save souls, therefore spend and be spent in this work.' 'Witness' and 'martyr' are the same word in the Greek, indicating the committed Christian's willingness to die for being a faithful witness.

THE PASTOR AS EVANGELIST

Secondly, there is the picture of the pastor doing the work of the evangelist. It is hard to distinguish the prime gift of the apostle Paul; though a church planter and pastor, he was always working as an evangelist. He said, 'Woe is me if I preach not the gospel.' He was the great New Testament writer, but he would not give his life simply to study and exposition. He was intimately involved in the lives and struggles of others. He wrote of ninety-nine different individuals in his letters; he prayed continually for them. Imitating his Saviour, he preached to the masses and dealt with individuals. We see this illustrated in Acts 18:4 where he sought publicly to win others to Christ, and shortly after in verses 7 and 8 he is privately leading Justus to Christ.

Paul wrote to Timothy, the pastor, and said, 'Do the work of the evangelist.' The pastor has many responsibilities – to feed the flock of God, to pray, to lead, to comfort, but *he must act as an evangelist also*. The pastor is to strive to lead souls to Christ, not only through the public ministry, but in one-to-one encounters. Faithful pastors will not content themselves in only building up a congregation and expounding the Scriptures to them, invaluable as this is. The pastor will also be burdened to see people being led to Christ in repentance and faith.

Robert Murray McCheyne preached in Dundee in Scotland in the early 1800s. Each Saturday he visited the dying in order to prepare his heart, so that on Sunday he might plead with souls the more earnestly. Yet, he said,

> I have not been like a shepherd after lost sheep, nor like a physician among dying men, nor like a servant bidding you to the marriage, nor like one plucking brands from the burning! How often have I gone to your houses to try and win souls, and you have put me off with a little worldly talk. I dared not tell you that you were perishing. How often have I sat at some of your tables and yearned for your souls, yet a false shame kept me silent! How often have I gone home crying bitterly, 'Free me from blood-guiltiness, O God!'

A pastor friend of mine who is a very fine Bible teacher goes outside his local supermarket two afternoons each week to give out tracts and talk to people about Christ. It is a vital work not only in terms of evangelism but also in keeping the pastor in touch with ordinary people.

Every pastor should try to develop his own strategy for doing the work of evangelism which includes, but goes beyond, preaching the gospel from a pulpit to a sympathetic crowd of hearers.

THE EVANGELIST

The third snapshot of evangelism we find in Acts is the appointed evangelist. The one individual named as an evangelist in the New Testament was Philip (Acts 21:8). He was not the most dynamic or charismatic of men. He was neither brash nor outspoken, but he is described as having a 'good reputation, full of the Holy Spirit and wisdom' (Acts 6:3).

In the fullest description of his work in Acts 8, we get a number of insights into the character and personality of this man. Philip was obedient to the Lord's leading (vv. 26-27); he was looking for opportunities (v. 28); he was led by the Holy Spirit (v. 29); he waited for guidance (v. 29); he was courteous (vv. 30-31); his approach was simple (vv. 32-34); he was scriptural (v. 35), and he looked for faith before publicly baptising new converts (v. 37).

The Bible lists qualities required for the recognizing and appointing of elders and deacons (1 Tim. 3:1-13 and Titus 1:5-9), but there is no specific list referring directly to the evangelist. However, early in the history of the church, a group of seven men were sought out, to ensure that the first Christian leaders could give themselves directly and continually to prayer and the ministry of the Word. Philip, the evangelist, was one of these seven men (Acts 6:1-7).

He was chosen by 'the whole multitude' and found to be acceptable by the apostles, who prayed for him (and the other six men), and then, in an act of identification, laid hands on him. We read that immediately after the 'Word of God spread, and the number of the disciples multiplied greatly in Jerusalem' (Acts 6:7). Philip was greatly used in preaching to large numbers of people in Samaria (Acts 8:5-8, 12), but he was also willing to be involved in patient personal work with an open Bible, as shown in his dealings with the Ethiopian (Acts 8:26-35). We in the West today also need to recognize and appoint those whose calling is to lead the work of evangelism in the church, undistracted by other responsibilities.

EXAMPLES OF THE EVANGELIST

Although Philip is the only person named as an evangelist, there were many more. Trevor Knight in his excellent book *God's Early Evangelists* describes some of the others:

- John the Baptist – 'the brief evangelist'
- Andrew – 'the personal evangelist'
- Peter – 'the pioneer evangelist'
- Philip – 'the freelance evangelist'
- Paul – ' the adaptable evangelist'
- John – 'the author evangelist'
- Anna – 'the woman evangelist'
- the Bethlehem shepherds – 'the unknown evangelists'
- Jesus – 'the divine evangelist'

However, the two outstanding evangelists of the New Testament are the Lord Jesus Christ and then the Apostle Paul. We have already looked at Christ's evangelistic work, but Paul, too, is a pattern for all Christians.

Paul never sought the attention or adoration of believers; Christ alone was to have the pre-eminence in all things (Col. 1:18). It was Paul who described himself as 'less than the least of all the saints' (poor grammar, but great theology!), and 'the chief' of sinners (Eph. 3:8; 1 Tim. 1:15). Paul is not 'The Word become flesh'. He did not die for us or rise again. Our blessed hope is not to look for his appearing in the sky. These things are reserved for Christ alone. But Paul would do anything so that Christ might be exalted (Phil. 1:20-24).

However, as Paul followed Christ, we should follow Paul (1 Cor. 11:1; Phil. 3:17;4:9; 2 Thess. 3:7 and 9). He is a pattern saint, and he is a pattern evangelistic worker.

The Lord had described Paul as 'a chosen vessel of Mine to bear My name before Gentiles, kings, and the children of Israel'

(Acts 9:15); and Paul saw himself as a steward of a ministry he received from God (1 Cor. 4:1, 2 and 7). His conversion was his calling into evangelism (2 Cor. 4:5-6). But his evangelism was more than the fulfilling of a sense of duty. He was deeply burdened; it was his life's work and passion. There was no sense of being on or off duty for he was 'always carrying about in the body the dying of the Lord Jesus, that the life of Jesus also may be manifested in our body' (2 Cor. 4:10). He could say, 'My heart's desire and prayer to God for Israel is that they may be saved' (Rom. 10:1). His words, 'as much as is in me' (Rom. 1:14-16), express his commitment to spreading the good news, and his feeling that he was a debtor to all, until he had discharged his duty and told them of the Saviour. Preaching Christ, he warned and taught every man using all his wisdom (Col. 1:28). Everything that happened to him was evaluated as to its effect on the proclamation of the gospel worldwide (cf. Phil. 1:12).

THE EVANGELIST'S MESSAGE

Paul's message ('my gospel' as he called it in Romans 2:16) is clear and concise: 'For Christ did not send me to baptize, but to preach the gospel, not with wisdom of words, lest the cross of Christ should be made of no effect...but we preach Christ crucified, to the Jews a stumbling block and to the Greeks foolishness but to those who are called...Christ the power of God and the wisdom of God' (1 Cor. 1:17; 23-24); 'For I determined not to know anything among you except Jesus Christ and Him crucified' (1 Cor. 2 :2); 'For we do not preach ourselves, but Christ Jesus the Lord, and ourselves your servants for Jesus' sake' (2 Cor. 4:5).

He grieved deeply when false teachers brought false gospels with wrong emphases (Gal. 1:8-9; 2 Cor. 11:13-15). Though totally uncompromising on his message, he was willing to adapt his style and methods to be appropriate and relevant to different audiences. This is demonstrable by comparing his approach to, for example, the Thessalonians in Acts 17:1-4 and the Athenians in Acts 17:16-34. He explained his reasoning for this in 1 Corinthians 9:19-23. Where no Bible knowledge could be assumed, Paul referred to God as Creator, and built his case for the gospel without the audience needing a working knowledge of the Old Testament. His approach was much more rooted in Bible knowledge for those who would have it. Paul knew the Word, and the world, and he was able to relate the Word to the world.

Paul practised accountability not only before God, but before others also, and so reported back at length to the church who had commissioned him (Acts 13:1-3; 14:26-28). His integrity is so transparent that he can and does appeal to it as a vindication of his position and authority: 'But we have renounced the hidden things of shame, not walking in craftiness nor handling the word of God deceitfully, but by manifestation of the truth commending ourselves to every man's conscience in the sight of God' (2 Cor. 4:2); and 'We give no offense in anything, that our ministry may not be blamed. But in all things we commend ourselves as ministers of God' (2 Cor. 6:3-6).

THE COST OF COMMITMENT

Such a high standard of commitment to the Lord, the lost and the Lord's people is costly. Paul spoke of being 'hard pressed on every side...perplexed...persecuted...struck down... always carrying about in the body the dying of the Lord Jesus' (2 Cor. 4:8-10). Later he listed some of his sufferings, describing awful experiences:

> ... in labours more abundant, in stripes above measure, in prisons more frequently, in deaths often. From the Jews five times I received forty stripes minus one. Three times I was beaten with rods; once I was stoned; three times I was shipwrecked; a night and a day

> I have been in the deep; in journeyings often, in perils of waters...of robbers...of my own countrymen...of the Gentiles...in the city...in the wilderness...in the sea...among false brethren, in weariness and toil, in sleeplessness often, in hunger and thirst, in fastings often, in cold and nakedness – besides the other things, what comes upon me daily: my deep concern for all the churches (2 Cor. 11:23-28).

Far from turning away from this, or indeed the Lord and His service, Paul sought to accept it all as a means of keeping himself faithful: 'I discipline my body and bring it into subjection, lest, when I have preached to others, I myself should become disqualified' (1 Cor. 9:27).

As far as money was concerned, in contrast to the false preachers of his day, Paul 'preached the gospel of God...free of charge' (2 Cor. 11:7). He evidently relied on other churches to give to his support (2 Cor. 11:8; Phil. 4:16), but set no fees and charged no admission to hear the gospel. For Paul, this was a basic principle which he explained in his first letter to the Corinthians (9:18): 'What is my reward then? That when I preach the gospel, I may present the gospel of Christ without charge, that I may not abuse my authority in the gospel.' For him, to charge to hear the gospel was an abuse of his calling and, therefore, of the gospel itself.

He did, however, ask for prayer and was not embarrassed to do so. At least seven times in his letters we find him urging others to pray for him (Rom. 15:30-32; 2 Cor. 1:11; Eph. 6:18-20; Phil. 1:19; Col. 4:3-4; 2 Thess. 3:1-3; Phil. 22; Heb. 13:18-19). Clearly his dependence was not upon men, but upon God (see 1 Corinthians 2:4 and 2 Corinthians 10:4-6). He had learned this from the very beginning. Writing his testimony to the Galatians, he said:

> But when it pleased God, who separated me from my mother's womb and called me through His grace, to reveal His Son in me, that I might preach Him among the Gentiles, I did not immediately confer with

> flesh and blood, nor did I go up to Jerusalem to those who were apostles before me; but I went to Arabia and returned again to Damascus. Then after three years I went up to Jerusalem (1:15-18).

For Paul, working as a pastor-evangelist, it seemed that nothing was too high to be attempted; nothing was too hard to be endured; nothing was too good to be hoped for, and nothing was too precious to give away. His motto might well have been, 'I have been crucified with Christ; it is no longer I who live, but Christ lives in me; and the life which I now live in the flesh I live by faith in the Son of God, who loved me and gave Himself for me' (Gal. 2:20).

ALL THINGS TO ALL PEOPLE

Immediately after his conversion, Paul 'preached the Christ in the synagogues, that He is the Son of God' (Acts 9:20) and that was to be the beginning of a pattern for his life. He used every legitimate method he could to preach the gospel. When writing his first letter to the persecuted church at Thessalonica, Paul sought to encourage the believers. He spoke repeatedly of faith, love and hope, encouraging them to wait eagerly for the second coming of Christ. In chapters 1 and 2 we see Paul as the evangelist and pastor to the people of that ancient city. The message, the minister, the ministry and the motive were all right, as he sought to win the people, not by manipulation but by communication.

Paul sought to make himself adaptable to reach each type of person with whom he could make contact. He wrote in 1 Corinthians 9:16-17, 'For if I preach the gospel, I have nothing to boast of, for necessity is laid upon me; yes, woe is me if I do not preach the gospel! For if I do this willingly, I have a reward.'

A SACRED STEWARDSHIP

It is clear that the life and character of the preacher is uppermost in the mind of Paul. If the best sermon is a holy life, Paul was a great preacher; but he was not content just to live, he also had to speak. He didn't merely tell people what they wanted to hear, so that they would do what he wanted them to do. Instead, he spoke the truth in love, believing firmly that his message was not something that man had made up, but the gospel of God (Gal. 1:11). For him, ministry was a sacred stewardship – 'approved by God to be entrusted with the gospel' (1 Thess. 2:4). His was not just a career, but a life with an all-consuming passion. He loved the Lord and he loved the lost. His desire and therefore his prayer was that they should be saved (see Rom. 10:1). In Acts 28, we see that Paul was evangelizing from morning until evening. He was not 'clocking in' or watching the time. Wesley's evangelists were described as men 'out of breath pursuing souls'. Paul fitted that description too.

His manner of proclamation and preaching is a standard and goal for evangelists today:

> Our gospel did not come to you in word only, but also in power, and in the Holy Spirit and in much assurance, as you know what manner of men we were among you for your sake.

> We were bold in our God to speak to you the gospel of God in much conflict. For our exhortation did not come from deceit, or uncleanness, nor was it in guile...not as pleasing men, but God who tests our hearts. For neither at any time did we use flattering words...nor a cloak of covetousness.... Nor did we seek glory from men....we were gentle among you, just as a nursing mother...we were well pleased to impart to you not only the gospel of God, but also our own lives...our labour and toil;...labouring night and day... devoutly and justly and blamelessly we behaved ourselves among you who believed (1 Thess. 1:5; 2:2-10).

The example has been lived out and a pattern set; now where are the people who will take hold of the torch and spread the light of the Lord Jesus wherever they go?

7 The uniqueness of the evangelist

Tucked away at the end of the biography of the life of Paul is an insight which perhaps more than any other explains the uniqueness of the gift of the evangelist. At long last Paul has arrived, under arrest, at the capital of the great Roman Empire. He was greeted warmly by the local believers, but was placed under house-arrest. He was there for 'two whole years in his own rented house, and received all who came to him, preaching the kingdom of God and teaching the things which concern the Lord Jesus Christ with all confidence, no one forbidding him' (Acts 28:30-31). '[M]any came to him at his lodging, to whom he explained and solemnly testified of the kingdom of God, persuading them concerning Jesus from both the Law of Moses and the Prophets, from morning till evening' (Acts 28:23).

The three verbs in this last verse describe the particular work and calling of the evangelist: *explained, testified, persuaded*. Satan, society and self have co-operated to blind and mislead men and women as to the essence of true religion. Something within people still believes that good works are the ticket to God and heaven, but nothing could be further from the truth (Eph. 2:8-9; Titus 3:8). We need to explain constantly how, because of the finished work of Christ, there is salvation by grace, through faith. Good pastors and Bible teachers, as well as evangelists, will want to communicate this. They will do so as simply, directly and earnestly as they can.

PROCLAIMING CHRIST CRUCIFIED

Paul declared, 'I determined not to know anything among you except Jesus Christ and Him crucified' (1 Cor. 2:2) and 'God forbid that I should glory except in the cross of our Lord Jesus Christ' (Gal. 6:14). The cross of Jesus Christ is both essential and central to any evangelistic preaching. The evangelist must not speak merely of forgiveness, but will always (I believe, without exception) explain the hidden work of Christ on the cross – how God laid all the sin of the world on Jesus (Isa. 53:6), the Just who died for the unjust (1 Pet. 3:18), being made sin for us all (1 Pet. 2:24).

It was the explanation of the cross which convinced me at the age of fifteen that I needed to trust Christ. It seemed clear that if God had loved me enough to send his 'only begotten Son' into the world to die for me, then the least I must do is trust Him. My simple, teenage logic was very biblical, although I didn't know it at the time:

> What shall I render to the LORD
> For all His benefits toward me?

> I will take up the cup of salvation,
> And call upon the name of the LORD. (Ps. 116:12-13)

Christ died for our sin, was buried, and on the glorious third day rose again from the dead. The stone which sealed the tomb of Christ, rolled away, not so much to let out Christ, but to let us look in and see the empty tomb. The world desperately needs to hear 'that Christ died for our sins according to the Scriptures, and that He was buried, and that He rose again the third day according to the Scriptures, and that He was seen...' (1 Cor. 15:3-5). All evangelists will want to explain the hidden work of Christ on the cross as He bore our sins in His body on the tree.

TESTIFYING TO THE POWER OF GOD

There is more to the work of the evangelist, however. The second verb is 'testify'. On three occasions in the book of Acts Paul shared a very comprehensive account of his conversion. Testifying to the truth, though, is more than just personal experience. It is commending the truth for what it is, namely, truth. My experience of it does not make it true; it is that by its very nature. Explaining the facts and their personal influence is a powerful weapon in the hands of the Lord. Experiences are always hard to refute, but impossible if solidly grounded on the Word of God. The evangelist, like others, will use personal testimony to drive home the truth and relevance of the claims of Christ. Our testimony is an adornment of the truth. It often gets the attention of the listener who is keen to have personal insights into the life and experiences of others.

PERSUADING PEOPLE TO BELIEVE

There will be other Christian workers involved in the ministry of 'explaining' and 'testifying', however. Thus it is that the unique dimension of the work and calling of the evangelist is seen in the third verb found in Acts 28:23 – 'persuading'. Paul's persuasion was not false emotion stirred by tear-jerking anecdotes and illustrations. It was biblical. He 'persuaded them from the Law of Moses and the Prophets'. Paul used the Old Testament as a bridge to Jesus Christ. Illustrations can be useful and illuminating; they can be the hook to capture people's attention, or the hammer to drive home truths; but they must not be the main stay of our message. Spurgeon likened illustrations to windows in a building, but then added that we don't want to construct only a greenhouse!

Paul's method described in Acts 28 when he was near the end of his life was one that he used consistently throughout his ministry. For example, he used the same pattern much earlier with the Thessalonians: 'Then Paul, as his custom was, went in to them and for three Sabbaths reasoned with them from the Scriptures, explaining and demonstrating that Christ had to suffer and rise again from the dead...and some of them were persuaded...' (Acts 17:2-4).

Evangelistic preaching at its finest and most useful refuses simply to outline and explain truth, but it appeals, applies and explains to the hearers how they can and must respond. John the Baptist preached and then, in answering general questions, replied specifically telling various groups what they must do (Luke 3:7-14). Jesus met the woman caught in the act of adultery, challenged her accusers, refused to condemn her and then told her specifically what she must do, before applying what he had done to the watching and listening crowd (John 8:2-12). On the day of Pentecost Peter followed the same pattern found in Acts 28:23: he explained the Word using the Law and the Prophets, testified and exhorted (persuaded) the people (Acts 2, particularly verse 40), and then he drove home the message as he explained 'what they must do' (2:38-41).

W. E. Vine in his *Expository Dictionary* says that the word 'persuade' means to 'prevail upon or win over...to bring about a change of mind by the influence of reason or moral considerations'. In some ways this is the most demanding part of a message. It is emotionally, spiritually and, therefore, physically draining. It is the nearest thing to strength departing from me that I ever feel in the work of evangelism. This part of a message is most likely to cause resistance and therefore criticism and even opposition. Satan will do his utmost to dissuade preachers from preaching for a verdict. For the evangelist, it is not enough to have been faithful in teaching the gospel, there has to be the earnestness of an application. Neither is it sufficient to say it is the Spirit's work to drive home the application. God in His grace commands us to 'preach the Word' and preaching will include application. The evangelist, particularly, will feel constrained to 'compel them to come in' (Luke 14:23) and to urge the listener to 'Choose for yourselves this day whom you will serve' (Josh. 24:15).

A MESSAGE FOR ALL

God alone is omniscient, and therefore the evangelist should 'cast the net wide'. Some time ago, I was preaching for a week in Fraserburgh in the north of Scotland. As a town, it is rich through fishing the seas. The fishermen, the last of the hunters, will go to sea for weeks or months at a time. Diligently they study and survey through sonic radar systems exactly where the fish are. Then they will shoot a net to cover the area of a soccer pitch, and maybe haul in a shoal of fish weighing up to 700 tonnes. It could be that the huge net may get caught and lost, but the possibility of a good catch makes the risk worthwhile. The evangelist as a 'fisher of men' (Matt. 4:19; Mark 1:17) will study and sacrifice to ensure that he is being as effective as is humanly possible, in catching many fish. 'The one that got away' will always be a grief to the evangelist's heart.

There is a constant sense that God may do something bigger than we could ever ask or think. Two verses in particular encourage me to appeal lovingly to men and women: 'The wind blows where it wishes, and you hear the sound of it, but cannot tell where it comes from and where it goes. So is everyone who is born of the Spirit' (John 3:8) and 'you do not know which will prosper, either this or that, or whether both alike will be good' (Eccles. 11:6). In the words of Jonathan to his armour-bearer, 'It may be that the LORD will work for us' (1 Sam. 14:6). Everything that counts has a cost, and nothing counts more than winning men and women to Christ for the glory of God. After all, God really 'desires all men to be saved and to come to the knowledge of the truth' (1 Tim. 2:4), so surely I should too!

George Whitefield died at the age of fifty-five years having worn himself out with a lifetime of evangelistic labours. On the last night of his life on earth he began to mount the stairs of the Presbyterian manse in Newbury, Massachusetts. As he did, he could hear the crowds outside begging him to preach the gospel one more time. On the landing, instead of going to bed, he turned and began to preach, holding a candle in his hand. The candle burned itself out in the socket and flickered for a last time. It was a lovely picture of a life which had a zealous burning for the souls of men and women. It is a striking challenge to all evangelists to devote themselves to the supreme task of glorifying God by proclaiming the gospel and to live out these words from the hymn 'O For a Thousand Tongues': 'Preach Him to all, and cry in death, "Behold, behold the Lamb."'

8 Biblical pictures of the evangelist

Such is the evangelistic concern of the Holy Spirit, that He who moved in the minds of the authors of the Bible, saw fit to illustrate and portray the work of the evangelist through many pictures. There are at least twenty-five pen portraits of the person who testifies to the Lord. Clearly, these pictures do not all apply specifically or uniquely to the evangelist, but they each give us insights into particular aspects of the work of the soul-winner.

A FISHERMAN (MATT. 4:19)

In Luke 5:1-11 we read how Christ taught the crowds from the vantage point of Simon's fishing boat. When Jesus had stopped speaking, he commanded Simon to 'Launch out into the deep and let down your nets for a catch.' The shoal of fish they caught was remarkable; Simon Peter realized his sinfulness in comparison with the authority and purity of Christ, and Christ used the opportunity to speak to Peter: 'Do not be afraid, from now on you will catch men' (Luke 5:10). The words, 'Follow me, and I will make you fishers of men' (Matt. 4:19) caught the imagination of Andrew and Peter, who were experienced fishermen. They knew the toil, hardship, patience and rewards of fishing in unpredictable seas. They were aware of the times of feverish activity and the times of quiet waiting. They knew the skills that should be developed in order to fish effectively, but their priorities were to be rearranged so they would realize the value of a person compared with a fish.

A SOLDIER (1 TIM. 1:18; 2 COR. 10:3-6)

The Roman Empire made its presence felt. Soldiers were a common sight. Their orderliness, dedication and discipline were known. Military metaphors proved to be a good source of illustrations for Paul as they were universally understood.

'For though we walk in the flesh, we do not war according to the flesh. For the weapons of our warfare are not carnal but mighty in God for pulling down strongholds, casting down arguments and every high thing that exalts itself against the knowledge of God...' (2 Cor. 10:3-5). Writing to Timothy, Paul says, 'You therefore must endure hardship as a good soldier of Jesus Christ. No one engaged in warfare entangles himself with the affairs of this life, that he may please him who enlisted him as a soldier' (2 Tim. 2:3-4). We need to be reminded that, as A. W. Tozer expressed it, we are living in a battleground, not a playground. Now is not the time for rest, relaxation and recreation, but for all-out war against the prince of the power of the world for the souls of men and women. Conscious of this John Wesley could say, 'Leisure and I have parted.'

A SOWER (1 COR. 3:7)

This picture of the evangelist is used in the Old Testament (Ps. 126:5-6; Eccles. 11:6), but was made more familiar by the Lord Jesus (Mark 4:26-29; Matt. 13:3-9, 18-23), and is applied by Paul in 1 Corinthians 3:6-8.

The sower is convinced that when the seed is sown, a secret work will be going on undetected by any onlookers whereby the seed is watered, nourished and grows. The sower has a confidence that in time a harvest will come: 'Let us not grow weary while doing good, for in due season we shall reap if we do not lose heart' (Gal. 6:9).

A MASTER BUILDER (1 COR. 3:9-11)

The Christian is pictured as a building (1 Cor. 3:9, 16-17), but the evangelist is not only a building, but a builder. Paul describes himself as 'a wise master builder' who has 'laid the foundation which another has built on' and warns 'let each take heed how he builds on it'. The building is to be of 'gold, silver, precious stones', not 'wood, hay and straw', and the promise is that 'if anyone's work which he has built on it endures, he will receive a reward' (1 Cor. 3:10-14). Motive, ministry and the minister are all tested and will be made manifest on the Great Day. God weighs up our motives: why we are evangelizing, who we are depending on for 'success' and who gets the glory when things go well.

A STEWARD (1 COR. 4:1-2)

The message which has been entrusted to us is the most wonderful news in the world. We cannot and must not keep it to ourselves. We have the gospel to declare, and an indebtedness to discharge. In 1 Corinthians 4:1-2, Paul says: 'Let a man so consider us, as servants of Christ and stewards of the mysteries of God. Moreover, it is required in stewards that one be found faithful.' The picture is repeated in Colossians 1:25 and in 1 Peter 4:10. We are challenged to be 'good stewards of the manifold grace of God', on the basis that we have received a gift from God.

A CARING PARENT (1 COR. 3:1-2)

Whatever Paul was, he was not a harsh preacher. His tender love and parent-like concern for those among whom he is labouring is seen in his description of his evangelistic and pastoral endeavours. Those converted through him he describes as 'my little children for whom I labour in birth ...' (Gal. 4:19). They were his 'babes in Christ' whom he 'fed ... with milk and not with solid food' (1 Cor. 3:1-2). Paul knew that young converts have to face the persecution and pressure of a hostile world, but to feed with milk, and then meat, will enable them to grow in the grace and the knowledge of Jesus Christ.

AN AMBASSADOR (2 COR. 5:20)

Ambassadors represent their own king or nation in another nation. The country in which they live is not their home; they are serving a different master. The way they live and the things they say and do are on behalf of someone else. Ambassadors do not involve themselves in the politics of the country where they are placed, but stand for the principles of their own kingdom. The illustration is clear: as citizens of the kingdom of heaven, we are living in this world, representing the Lord of heaven. 'We are ambassadors for Christ' (2 Cor. 5:20; Eph. 6:20; Rom. 10:15).

A TRAINED ATHLETE (1 COR. 9:24 AND 2 TIM. 2:5)

Most generations have been fascinated by the dedication and commitment of men and women who put aside present pleasure for the sake of disciplining and developing their skills and abilities to win in sport or athletics. There is intensity and concentration so that the athlete might be trained and be qualified to compete. Running to win is the picture used to portray the Christian who earnestly seeks to serve Christ.

A SHEPHERD (JOHN 10:7-18; LUKE 15:3-7)

Ira Sankey popularized the hymn,

> There were ninety and nine that safely lay
> In the shelter of the fold,
> But one was out on the hills away,
> Far off from the gates of gold –
> Away on the mountains wild and bare,
> Away from the tender Shepherd's care,
> Away from the tender Shepherd's care.

The idea was not originally his! The Lord pictured Himself and His followers in turn as being like shepherds searching for, finding and rescuing lost sheep. To what lengths will a good shepherd go to in order that one lost sheep might be found!

AN OX TREADING OUT THE CORN (1 COR. 9:9)

It was written in the Law of Moses that the mouth of the ox was not to be muzzled as it trod out the corn. The command not only showed God's care for oxen, but for Christian workers, who may be carrying heavy burdens, and using their strength to work hard, but who need to be cared for.

THE FILTH AND EXCREMENT OF THE WORLD (1 COR. 4:13)

This is not the most flattering picture of the evangelist! Opposition, persecution and pressure are promised to the believer. The evangelist is not going to be an exception to this. Often he will be seen as the filth of the world, and the offscouring of all things unto this day.

SERVANTS OF CHRIST (EZRA 5:11; 2 COR. 4:5; EXOD. 21:1-6)
The Lord treats us as His friends. We are His sons and daughters. Nevertheless, our sense of indebtedness to Him is such that we feel we are His servants, and the servants of others for Jesus' sake. Our rights have been yielded to Him. We are here on earth to do His bidding, wherever and however He wants. We feel our one responsibility is to please our Master. Philip the evangelist exemplified this when he left Samaria, at the Lord's command, to go into the desert where he was directed to the Ethiopian eunuch.

A DEBTOR PAYING BACK HIS DEBT (ROM. 1:14)
We can never out-give God. We feel debtors to Him, but also to the lost around us whoever they are – Greeks, Barbarians, wise and unwise. We will want all the people we meet to hear about Christ who gives hope to the very worst. Our witness is an expression of gratitude to God for all He has done for us.

A GUARD KEEPING THE GOSPEL SAFE (1 TIM. 6:20)
A prison guard should be very watchful. For the Roman guard, a prisoner escaping would lead to the guard himself suffering the same punishment that the prisoner was due to endure. The incentive to keep the prisoner secure was great! The Bible makes it clear that there is a duty to defend the faith, not allowing the love of novelty to cause us to deviate from the truth. The central themes of Christianity are not negotiable.

AN EARTHEN VESSEL FULL OF TREASURE (2 COR. 4:7)
The excellency of the power of the gospel is from God and not of us. There is treasure in these earthen vessels of our bodies, and anything good and eternal in us is from God. All that we are naturally is temporary, but everything which lasts for ever is of God and therefore to be used for his glory.

A DYING MAN (2 COR. 4:16)

Physically, we will increasingly recognize our own frailties, but inwardly we should be growing stronger, as our daily communion with the Lord will build up the part of our being which is most vital. While I have time, let me live and speak out for Christ.

A CHURCH ROBBER (2 COR. 11:8)

Paul describes himself, ironically, as a 'church robber', for he was willing to receive gifts and help from other churches that he might continue in the work of evangelism. He did not take the generous support of others for granted, and sought to be a faithful steward of his money and time. He was working on their behalf, and they were very much a part of his ministry and achievements through their involvement (Phil. 4:15-17).

A DEMOLITION CONTRACTOR (GAL. 2:18)

Like Jeremiah, Paul knew what it was to destroy before he could build effectively (cf. Jer. 1:9-10). It has been well said that we have to get people lost before they can be saved. Sometimes people's false belief-systems have to be destroyed before it is possible to rebuild a biblical view of God, themselves and salvation. In certain religions, it is all too easy to tag on the Lord Jesus as just another god.

AN OPHTHALMOLOGIST (EPH. 3:9)

The spiritually blind receive their sight when the gospel is preached. The new convert will see the world very differently, as George Wade Robinson describes in his hymn 'Loved with everlasting love':

> Heaven above is softer blue,
> Earth around is sweeter green;

> Something lives in every hue
> Christless eyes have never seen.

A GIFT GIVEN TO THE CHURCH (EPH. 4:11-12)

'And He Himself gave some to be apostles, some prophets, some evangelists, and some pastors and teachers, for the equipping of the saints for the work of the ministry, for the edifying of the body of Christ ...' The church is the heart concern of Christ. He gives to His church evangelists. Church leadership which ignores or rejects God's gift in the form of the evangelist, not only hinders the evangelistic outreach of the church, but hinders the equipping and edifying of the church.

A PATTERN, MOULD OR EXAMPLE (1 COR. 4:16; 11:1; PHIL. 3:17)

Christians still notice the example set by other believers, and follow it. The evangelist in a church will help to make the church membership more evangelistic. The best way I know of helping Christians get a burden for lost souls, is for them to be with evangelists and/or to be involved in evangelism.

A LABOURER (IN PRAYER) (COL. 4:12)

Every evangelist is grateful for the prayer support of others. It has been pointed out that when Billy Graham stood up to preach at one of his crusades, he was the most prayed for man, in the most prayed for place on earth. Nevertheless, the evangelist must be a person of prayer in his own right. Epaphras was a prayer warrior, as he fervently prayed for others. The evangelist is to be known for praying as well as preaching.

A TEACHER (HEB. 5:12)

It is expected that each Christian is to grow to be a teacher of the Word of God, and the evangelist is to be no exception. In proclaiming the gospel there is inevitably an aspect of teaching.

The evangelist is teaching vital truths of eternal significance to people who are ignorant. This makes the work of the evangelist to be one of many general benefits to society at large.

A FRAGRANCE (2 COR. 2:14-16)

What a lovely description of the evangelist: diffusing the fragrance of his knowledge in every place. That is something to aspire to, and to be. Sadly, to some, we are an aroma of death, though to others we are an aroma of life.

These many Bible illustrations of the evangelist demonstrate what the Lord wants to drive home to readers of the Bible: God is concerned for the lost, so He sent his Son to be the Saviour. Now constrained by this love, believers in general and evangelists in particular are burdened to get out the gospel message.

Thinking of this I am reminded of the Mercedes Benz television advertisement promoting their energy-absorbing car body. Their design had evidently been copied by other companies because of its success, yet when asked why Mercedes Benz didn't enforce their patent, a company spokesman replies: 'Because some things in life are too important not to share.'

9 A great cloud of witnesses

The clarion call of the Great Commission has been heard by Christian people through twenty centuries of church history. The Lord Jesus said: 'Go therefore and make disciples of all nations, baptizing them in the name of the Father and of the Son and of the Holy Spirit, teaching them to observe all things that I have commanded you...' (Matt. 28:19-20). It was Jesus who said, 'As the Father has sent Me, I also send you', and 'Go into all the world and preach the gospel to every creature' (John 20:21; Mark 16:15).

In giving the command, He also imparted the ability to obey and fulfil the commission. All believers are to be involved in this work, and evangelists have been at the forefront. Throughout twenty centuries the work of the evangelist, spreading the good news into previously darkened areas, has been greatly valued.

EARLY EVANGELISTS

The early Christian historian, Eusebius, wrote of travelling preachers who, in the first century after Jesus' ascension, carried the gospel from marketplace to synagogue, from homes to amphitheatres throughout the Roman Empire, with great Holy Spirit zeal.

This body of evangelists grew during the second and third centuries, as they took advantage of the political unity of the Roman Empire and the widespread use of Greek as a trade language. Most well-known was Chrysostom who evangelized with great effect throughout the Middle East. But there were many others, such as Gregory of Thaumaturgus who began to preach in Pontus when there was only a tiny nucleus of believers in that city. A generation later, at the time of his death, there were only a few dozen who were *not* Christians.

In the third century, nomadic tribes invaded Europe, and Roman Christians were among the captives taken. Ulphilas, a descendant of these slaves, evangelized the Goths and translated the Scriptures into their language, and Christian assemblies were planted throughout the area. Gothic evangelists in turn took the gospel to barbarian tribes across Europe. Men of God, such as Cyprian in Carthage and Martin of Tours in France, were used mightily as instruments of the Lord, and changed the whole course of civilization. Others were notable for their work in evangelising whole nations. Bede and Augustine in England, Patrick in Ireland, Columba in Scotland and Cuthbert in Scandinavia are good examples.

Sadly, the church in these times was often compromising, weak and worldly. Outward ritual replaced the inward relationship with God, which is the essence of Christian experience. Purity of doctrine was no longer regarded as paramount. It was in such a setting that Islam arose in the seventh century. Its influence spread rapidly. The sword was used both to spread Islam and to seek to stop its growth. Replacing the sword of the Word with the sword of warriors, and the preaching of the blood of Christ by shedding the blood of others did not further the cause of the gospel. Such is the lesson of the Crusades.

Neither military crusades, nor verbal battles win precious souls to Christ. Francis of Assisi and Raymond Lull sought lovingly to reach Moslems for Christ. When Francis preached Christ to the Sultan of Egypt in 1219, the Moslem monarch said, 'If I were to meet any more Christians like you, I would become a Christian.' However, the reception amongst Islamic people has not always been so welcoming. Lull's tearful attempts to evangelize Africans were rewarded by his twice being deported; and on his third evangelistic journey, at the age of eighty, he was stoned to death.

Wherever culture and religion become merged, the community, humanly speaking, becomes harder to reach. Prayerful, patient, loving witness is God's chosen means of evangelization.

EARLY WESTERN EVANGELISTS

John Wycliffe was born in Richmond in Yorkshire, England, in the fourteenth century. Known as 'the morning star of the Reformation', he was not only the first man to translate the Bible into English, but he set about the evangelizing of the pagan masses in England. He gathered a group of 'poor preachers' called Lollards who began itinerant ministries around Britain and beyond, reading the Scriptures and preaching the gospel to the common people in the language they understood.

Wycliffe influenced others such as John Hus in Eastern Europe and Savonarola in Italy. Savonarola won tens of thousands to Christ, but was martyred by being hanged and burned in the city square of Florence.

THE REFORMATION AND LATER

A host of mighty evangelists and Bible teachers were raised up during the period of the Reformation: John Calvin, Martin Luther, Ulrich Zwingli, Menno Simons, John Smyth and John Knox are well known. John Calvin was the mastermind behind a great evangelistic thrust into France in 1555. Eighty-eight men from a cross-section of society were sent to France to evangelize, having been equipped with spiritual food and training under Calvin and others in Geneva. Martin Luther called himself 'an unworthy evangelist of our Lord Jesus Christ'. He equated Reformation and evangelism saying, 'If I should want to boast, I should glory in God that I am one of the apostles and evangelists in German lands, even though the devil and all his bishops and tyrants do not want me to be such.'

In the seventeenth century, at the time of the Puritans, John Bunyan from Bedford, England, was called to preach to Christians and also to the unsaved. He said that people 'came to hear the word by hundreds and that from all parts' and he 'thanked God that He gave unto me some measure of compassion and pity for their souls'. Reflecting on his work he said 'he dared not just speak the first word that came into his head, but sought out a word from God which [did] speak to, grip and awaken the conscience of the masses of the people'. He explains, 'I did preach what I did feel, what I did smartingly feel.'

It is to John Bunyan that we owe the most delightfully challenging picture of the evangelist. The words are from his masterly *Pilgrim's Progress* and some are engraved upon his statue in the centre of Bedford: 'Christian saw the picture of a very grave person hung up against the wall; and this was the fashion of it. He had eyes lifted up to heaven, the best of books was in his hand, the law of truth was written upon his lips, and the world was behind his back. He stood as if he pleaded with men and a crown of gold did hang over his head.'

Later on in *Pilgrim's Progress*, when Christian came into the house of the Interpreter, he was shown a picture of the evangelist: 'The man whose picture this is,' said the Interpreter, 'is one of a thousand; he can beget children, travail in birth with children and nurse them himself when they are born.'

Despite the Reformation and the Puritan era, the church in Europe became increasingly institutionalized, and needed to be resurrected into the life of the Lord Jesus. Count Nikolaus von Zinzendorf and a band of Moravians became evangelists to the world. It is said that the Moravians even sold themselves into slavery because that was the only effective way to reach the slaves with the gospel.

EIGHTEENTH-CENTURY REVIVAL
Then emerged John and Charles Wesley. Charles, as well as being a powerful evangelist himself, was to write Christian hymns (over 7,000 of them). His own journal sets his hymns in the context of daily ministerial duties including extensive travel and preaching four or five sermons a day. He combined mass-evangelism with spiritual conversations and searching personal interviews by night.

John pre-eminently preached the gospel. Although John said, 'the world is my parish', he did not leave the shores of Britain after 1738. In sixty years of itinerant evangelizing, John rode over 250,000 miles on horseback, preached over 40,000 times and, with a group of other evangelists, changed the tone and course of a nation, as hundreds of thousands of people were converted, churches established and a denomination founded.

At the same time, evangelist *par excellence*, George White-field was preaching and seeing great fruit in Britain and North America. Other notable names include Thomas Coke, Francis Asbury, John Cennick, Howel Harris, Christmas Evans, Daniel

Rowland, Benjamin Ingham, William Grimshaw, John Nelson and the Dutch American, Theodore Frelinghuysen. Wesley's evangelists were described as men 'out of breath pursuing souls'.

J. C. Ryle says of these evangelists:

> The men who wrought deliverance...were a few individuals, most of them clergymen, whose hearts God touched about the same time in various parts of the country. They were not wealthy or highly connected. They were not put forward by any church, party, society or institution. They were simply men whom God stirred up and brought out to do his work in the old apostolic way, by becoming evangelists of their day. They taught one set of truths. They taught them in the same way, with fire, reality, earnestness, as men fully convinced of what they taught. They taught them in the same spirit, always loving, compassionate and, like Paul, even weeping, but always bold, unflinching and not fearing the face of man. And they taught them on the same plan, always acting on the aggressive; not waiting for sinners to come to them, but going after and seeking sinners, not sitting idle till sinners offered to repent, but assaulting the high places of ungodliness like men storming a breach, and giving sinners no rest so long as they stuck to their sins.

At the same time, the Colonial Revival was taking place in New England through Jonathan Edwards, and elsewhere in America the gospel was being preached to great effect. Samuel Davies evangelized backcountry whites, Indians and Negroes in the Southern states. Only two years before the conversion of John Wesley, Isaac Watts the great English evangelical heard of the revival in New England and wrote: 'Never did we hear or read, since the first ages of Christianity, any event of this kind...it gives us further encouragement to pray and wait, and hope for the like display of His power in the midst of us.' This proved to be an encouragement for George Whitefield to cross the Atlantic on more than a dozen itinerant preaching missions, working through New England and other Colonies, drawing crowds of up to 40,000 people at a single meeting.

The long-term repercussions for good of that eighteenth-century revival were immense, widespread and long lasting. From these times of evangelism came great missionary endeavour from both North America and Great Britain; and in Britain there followed a wave of social reform pioneered by evangelicals, such as William Wilberforce (the abolition of slavery), Lord Shaftesbury (reform of the child labour and factory laws), John Howard and Elizabeth Fry (prison reform), as well as Dr Barnardo and George Muller (establishment of orphanages). Even the founding of trade unions and the British Labour Party had their origins in the people converted through the eighteenth-century revivals. The evangelistic work of people like William Carey, Adoniram Judson, James Hudson Taylor and David Livingstone is almost legendary. (I have often found that to read their biographies is to experience being sharpened in my burden for the lost, and to be fired again with evangelistic fervour.) Of course, names of great evangelists and missionaries are the tip of the iceberg; the unsung heroes and heroines are noted in heaven and they will receive their eternal reward over and above the knowledge of what they have been able to accomplish while here on earth.

CONTINUED GROWTH IN THE NINETEENTH CENTURY

The nineteenth century continued to see evangelistic endeavour in the West and missionary expansion worldwide. A mighty body of inter-church and denominational missionary societies was born, and valiant, often costly work was done, taking the gospel to the four corners of the earth. Asahel Nettleton, born in 1783, was among the first in the New World to spend the whole of his time as an itinerant evangelist. He held preaching missions in churches, whilst doing door-to-door personal work and counselling many souls. He was cautious and careful never to engage in fanaticism or extravagance of any kind. Being an intellectual and fairly melancholic, as well as maintaining decorum and extreme reserve in ministry, he did not readily fit into the usual mould of the evangelist! However, God used him.

Lorenzo Dow, also a New Englander, was very different. In upstate New York, he scolded the masses for being 'the offscouring of the earth'. He tried to copy John the Baptist, but was eccentric, mystical, highly strung and emotionally explosive. However, travelling from Louisville, Kentucky, to the New England area, tens of thousands repented of their sins and joined hastily built log cabins and stone masoned churches. Later Charles Finney was to come from the same area. There have been criticisms of some of Finney's methods; but his powerful logic, coupled with persuasive, dynamic oratory, drew vast crowds to hear his preaching, and many people were converted.

Many followed in this evangelistic trail in America; but it was left to D. L. Moody to capture the hearts of the common people on a vast scale at the end of the nineteenth century. He was a giant among evangelists, although he had little formal education. A converted shoe salesman who began evangelizing in Sunday school work, he teamed up with singer Ira Sankey. It was in Great Britain where he was first catapulted to great fame, but on both sides of the Atlantic he managed to bring Christians of all denominations together to co-operate in area-wide evangelistic campaigns. He was willing to use churches, theatres, halls and even a circus tent as venues where he could preach to people who would not normally go to Christian meetings. As well as preaching to huge crowds, he was a fine personal worker. He spoke to at least one unconverted person about Christ each day. It is said that he personally led 70,000 individuals to Christ. His one desire was to be a soul winner.

He said, 'I look upon this world as a wrecked vessel. God has given me a lifeboat and said to me, "Moody, save all you can."' Although blunt and brusque, he loved people, and they knew it.

Moody's successor, Reuben Archer Torrey, was a complete contrast. Both he and J. Wilbur Chapman were more educated and refined and, though much blessed, did not command the same attention as Moody. R. A. Torrey said, 'I would rather win souls than be the greatest king or emperor on earth; I would rather win souls than be the greatest general that ever commanded an army; I would rather win souls than be the greatest poet, or novelist, or literary man who ever walked this earth. My one ambition in life is to win as many as possible. Oh, it is the only thing worth doing, to save souls.'

Working in Britain at the time of Moody was C. H. Spurgeon. Converted at the age of fifteen, four years later he was pastor of one of London's most influential churches. As a young man, his oratory was exceptional, but thoroughly biblical and evangelistic. The number of his published sermons amounted to 3,800, with an estimated circulation of 300 million copies in all. During the four decades of his ministry, 14,000 new members were added to his church. He set up an evangelists' association and encouraged, trained and supported young men in their evangelistic and pastoral work. He experienced something of a real revival whilst ministering at the Metropolitan Tabernacle, London.

Spurgeon said:

Even if I were utterly selfish and had no care for anything but my own happiness, I would choose, if I might, under God, to be a soulwinner, for never did I know perfect, overflowing, unutterable happiness of the purest and most ennobling order, till I first heard of one who had sought and found the Saviour through my means.

> I recollect the thrill of joy that went through me! No young mother
> ever rejoiced so much over her first-born child, no warrior was so
> exultant over a hard-won victory!

MORE RECENT EVANGELISTS

Though theologically very different, William Booth and the Salvation Army made great inroads into the hearts of ordinary people in Britain. With his wife Catherine, who was herself a preacher, they together used popular military terminology to describe their work and workers. Salvationists were often attacked physically while preaching, money was scarce and difficulties innumerable; but still they went for souls, and went for the worst, and saw many remarkable instances of lives transformed by the power of the gospel. In 1904, aged seventy-five, 'General' Booth did a twenty-nine day 'automobile evangelistic tour' of Britain – 1,224 miles and 164 meetings long. He died in 1912 having travelled five million miles, preached nearly 60,000 sermons and drawn some 16,000 officers to serve in the Salvation Army.

Across the Atlantic, Billy Sunday, who had been a professional baseball player, made an immense impact. He was an orphan and had little formal education, but as an evangelist was energetic and dramatic. A colourful communicator, nobody could be left feeling indifferent about the gospel after hearing him. It is estimated that one million people responded to his gospel invitation.

In Japan, Paul Kanamori saw 43,000 professions of faith in his campaigns between 1916 and 1919. In India, Sadhu Sundar Singh, after an amazing conversion, was evangelizing in his home country and Ceylon; Jonathan Goforth and John Sung saw great fruit in China, and in Latin America evangelists such as Solomon Ginsburg, G. P. Howard, Joaquin Vela, Harry Strachan, Luis Palau and Nilson Fanini have all had effective ministry in reaching the lost. This century has seen great results in Africa also as a result of direct preaching evangelism.

W. P. Nicholson was converted in 1899 after a wild career as a seaman and railroad labourer in South Africa. His evangelistic missions in Ireland saw thousands converted, particularly amongst working men. 'W. P.' (like D. L. Moody before him) led a university mission to Cambridge which had a profound effect and stirred many educated young men to missionary work overseas; a remarkable example of God's ability to take an ordinary man and use him greatly in evangelism. He has on his gravestone the words of John 10:41-42 (KJV), originally written about John the Baptist: 'John did no miracle: but all things that John spake of this man were true. And many believed on him there.'

Some have deliberately sought to reach a particular class of people. The converted gypsy turned evangelist, Gypsy Smith, said that he wanted to preach the gospel in terms so that the man at the factory floor could understand it. Pastor F. W. Robertson was called the 'friend of the working-man' and yet he was very cultured and refined. He was asked about this and answered by saying, 'My tastes are with the aristocracy, but my principles are with the mob.'

Undoubtedly, the most prominent of all recent evangelists has been Billy Graham. He has attracted criticism because of his ecumenical links; but nevertheless in his work he has faithfully preached the gospel to over 100 million people in more than 100 countries. More than one million have recorded decisions (the Billy Graham Evangelistic Association would not claim that all these are actual conversions) for Christ in his public meetings, with many more responding to the gospel through radio, television, films and the printed page. Billy Graham was so concerned to see these people well grounded in the Word that he enlisted Dawson Trotman of the Navigators to devise courses to help establish new converts.

INTER-CHURCH EVANGELISM

The twentieth century has seen the growth of a number of effective, inter-church evangelistic organizations. Their work has often been more specialized than that of a local church that has its own responsibilities. Sometimes the inter-denominational work has arisen out of a frustration that established church work has neglected the needs of those outside a church. Mutual respect is vital, and involvement with such groups should not lead to a diminishing of involvement with the church whose emphasis will be on the preaching of the Word, prayer and worship as well as evangelism. Inter-church work often has a respect and credibility which a denominational church may not have in the eyes of the unconverted world. This has led to many opportunities, for example in missionary endeavour, or youth work or even in the placing of Bibles in hotels.

Several inter-denominational organizations whose emphasis is evangelism, stand out in our thinking. We thank God that He has raised up groups specializing in evangelism that complement the work of the church, but that are broader than one fellowship or denomination. I believe it is demeaning to call them para-church organizations, for many have done a magnificent work in reaching people in a way that would be too specialized for an ordinary local church. Such groups should, and usually do, work in unity with the church and should be seen as friends, never competitors.

As with denominations, it is imperative that current leadership maintains the evangelistic thrust that burdened their leaders. The Children's Special Service Mission began in 1867. It ran children's missions at seaside resorts. Eventually it became known as Scripture Union and broadened into a worldwide organization. Hudson Pope, one of its great children's evangelists, felt concerned that they would lose their evangelistic burden. In his last message to their annual conference he pleaded for them to keep their evangelistic emphasis and aim. We feel grateful to God for groups which have maintained their evangelistic thrust, and in so doing have often provided the setting for evangelists to work without the responsibilities involved in developing their own evangelistic organization.

Young Life, founded in Britain in 1911, has been used to reach countless thousands of young people. Its founders, Fred and Arthur Wood were powerful evangelists in their day, and having won young people to the Lord, trained many to be evangelists and missionaries in their own right. From it grew the European outreach, United Beach Missions. Jim Reyburn took Young Life to the USA where today it works mainly in schools. Also in the USA Youth for Christ deals mainly with teenagers and has been used to win thousands of young people to Christ. Its influence spread throughout the world. There are many other organizations such as InterVarsity Fellowship (called the Universities' and Colleges' Christian Fellowship in the UK), the Navigators, Girl Crusader Union, the Gideons, Child Evangelism Fellowship, Campus Crusade, Word of Life (founded by Jack Wyrtzen, a great evangelist in his own right), and Operation Mobilization (started by George Verwer). Each has made a major impact, thrusting (mainly young people) into evangelistic endeavour. One disappointment is that each organization, and indeed denomination, has its own inner circle of speakers, which excludes fine people from other groups. This reflects both a lack of trust and possibly love.

Rescue missions, as well as city and town missions, have done a great work in taking the gospel to urban and downtown areas. They have been used of the Lord, especially in reaching 'broken earthenware' and helping these people not only to faith, but faithfulness in life. They have balanced social involvement with evangelistic work in an impressive way.

Radio has been able to overcome political barriers and proclaim the gospel to literally millions. It is no cliché to say that eternity alone will reveal how many have been converted and helped spiritually through radio ministries. At present, Britain remains the only democracy in the world where Christians by law cannot purchase time on television or radio. For those countries where there is Christian radio, it is an inestimable blessing to be able to listen to Bible teaching hour after hour. Charles Fuller, one of the pioneers of this type of work, said, 'I'm not interested in figures. I'm interested in souls. Some people say I reach twenty million people. I don't know. All I know is that I preach the greatest message in the world. There may be greater orators, but nobody can preach a greater message because I preach from the world's greatest Book.... It is the old gospel, the simple gospel that draws people.'

There are also Christian film makers who provide a valuable evangelistic tool for reaching vast numbers of people. In less-developed countries a film or video can still attract substantial crowds of people to a large-screen showing.

> Therefore we also, since we are surrounded by so great a cloud of witnesses, let us lay aside every weight, and the sin which so easily ensnares us, and let us run with endurance the race that is set before us, looking unto Jesus, the author and finisher of our faith (Heb. 12:1-2).

May we share the vision that Frank Houghton describes in his hymn, 'Facing a task unfinished':

> We bear the torch that flaming
> Fell from the hands of those
> Who gave their lives proclaiming
> That Jesus died and rose.
> Ours is the same commission
> The same glad message ours,
> Fired by the same ambition,
> To Thee we yield our powers.

10 An earnest plea for evangelists

In tracing the theme of the evangelist through the Bible and history, it is clear that God has consistently set aside people for the task of reaching out to the lost with the gospel.

All Christian people have the joy of rubbing shoulders daily with the unconverted. It is a thrill and privilege to be able to share the Lord Jesus with them. One-to-one friendship evangelism seems, at present, to be the most effective way of winning people to Christ. We are with men and women for whom we can pray, to whom we can witness; and in God's good time, we trust, we will be able to win them for Christ. Being an evangelist in one's locality or place of work, or with family and friends is a duty indeed.

However, realistically, we are only touching a small minority of people through this method, and frankly most of those will be people of similar habits to ourselves. Perhaps this is why much of evangelicalism is fairly middle class. Who reaches those who do not have Christian friends? There are people who sleep when we are awake and rise when we sleep – who evangelizes them? 'Cold contacting' is looked down on, but it is better than leaving people unevangelized.

My plea is for the setting aside of gifted believers to be devoted to the full-time work of evangelism, in the same way that pastors and missionaries are appointed for their task. They will spearhead evangelistic endeavour in their locality and beyond. Their emphasis will be the proclaiming of the gospel. Christ crucified will be their abiding theme.

In recent years, great effort has been made by Christians to reform the laws of the land. But neither the Supreme Court in the USA nor the Parliament in Britain should be expected to do the Lord's work for us. As Christians, we are not the world's protesters but the Lord's proclaimers. The way to change society is heart-by-heart, one-by-one.

The lost state of men and women is more important than political change and endeavour. Every individual has an eternal existence and, outside of Christ, each is without hope both for time and eternity. There is an urgent need to 'rescue the perishing' while there is still time. If we let the opportunity slip, nobody else will ever be able to evangelize them. This is a task all Christians should be involved in, and strategically, we need to do all we can to remedy the desperate spiritual situation of men and women.

EVANGELISM AND THE LOCAL CHURCH

The local church is the vital factor here. For too long churches have continued a programme which seeks to meet the needs of its congregation, but is haphazard in trying to influence the community around. There need be no tension between congregation and community. We will have a salty influence on society if we are honestly and thoroughly seeking to be involved in every area of the locality. It is both fascinating and challenging to realize how many micro-communities within the larger community are willing and happy to have the input of winsome, non-threatening Christians. This is especially true when they represent a local church that is known for its sane Christian influence.

There are many strategies the churches and Christian fellowships should follow, but in the remit of this book, I want to make six specific suggestions:

1. CHURCHES SHOULD PRAY FOR MORE EVANGELISTS

Jesus said: "Do you not say, 'There are still four months and then comes harvest'? Behold, I say to you, lift up your eyes and look at the fields, for they are already white for harvest!" (John 4:35).

Matthew recalls (9:35-38) how,

> Jesus went about all the cities and villages, teaching in their synagogues, preaching the gospel of the kingdom, and healing every sickness and every disease among the people. But when He saw the multitudes, He was moved with compassion for them, because they were weary and scattered, like sheep having no shepherd. Then He said to His disciples, "The harvest truly is plentiful, but the labourers are few. Therefore pray the Lord of the harvest to send out labourers into His harvest."

Christ was saying that the great needs of today can be met only by prayer and people. The harvest is so great that labourers are needed. What a blessing it is when a church (or fellowship) and a locality has an evangelist. According to Ephesians 4:11-12, there will be evangelists in the church, placed and given by God himself: 'And He Himself gave... some evangelists...for the equipping of the saints for the work of ministry, for the edifying of the body of Christ...' The evangelist will have 'honour and dishonour...evil report and good report' and will be regarded as a 'deceiver and yet true, as unknown, and yet well known...as sorrowful, yet always rejoicing; as poor, yet making many rich; as having nothing and yet possessing all things' (2 Cor. 6:8-10). The evangelist will have the burden and ability to relate to the unsaved world around, without becoming like them and adopting their ways. Holiness (not monasticism) will characterize his life, as he spends time with unconverted people, seeking to reach them for Christ.

Evangelists, by their very nature, are deeply concerned for the souls of men and women. They have 'seen' something of the love of God to a lost world, and the thought that it means nothing to the many who pass by grieves the true evangelist. Love for God and the love of God constrains the evangelist to proclaim Christ (2 Cor. 5:14).

The evangelist is also aware of impending judgment. He feels it for himself and asks, 'What will I say at the judgment seat of Christ if I have not pleaded with men and women to repent and believe?' 'Knowing, therefore, the terror of the Lord, we persuade men' (2 Cor. 5:11). The evangelists feel their own indebtedness and responsibility. But the evangelist also asks, 'What will they say if I have not pleaded with them to be saved?' Ezekiel was called to be a watchman-evangelist:

> But if the watchman sees the sword coming and does not blow the trumpet, and the people are not warned, and the sword comes and takes any person from among them, he is taken away in his iniquity; but his blood I will require at the watchman's hand ... When I say to the wicked, "O wicked man, you shall surely die!" and you

do not speak to warn the wicked from his way, that wicked man shall die in his iniquity; but his blood I will require at your hand (Ezek. 33:6 and 8).

Is our call any different from Ezekiel's? So grave is the situation of impending judgment, how can sinners carry on obliviously? (Ezek. 21:10).

'To be a true minister to men,' said Phillips Brooks, 'is always to accept new happiness and new distress, both of them forever deepening and entering into closer and more inseparable union with each other the more profound and spiritual the ministry becomes. The man who gives himself to other men can never be a wholly sad man; but no more can he be a man of unclouded gladness.'

Under God, the gospel message proclaimed by the evangelist will be particularly used to precipitate a desire for the Lord in the heart of the hearer. The sense that what is proclaimed is indeed a message from God will be the conviction of preacher and, one trusts, hearer alike. The evangelist will be used of God to compel people to come to Christ. The evangelist will not be satisfied to present truth simply on a 'take it or leave it basis'. The message will have an urgent plea for sinners to repent and believe the gospel. The evangelist will be looking for the fruit of souls being truly converted as God uses the preaching. There will be an expression of heart and feelings as well as truth and information.

C. H. Spurgeon expressed this in his classic book, *Lectures to my Students*:

> The class requiring logical argument is small compared with the number of those who need to be pleaded with, by way of emotional persuasion. They require not so much reasoning as heart-argument, which is logic set on fire. You must argue with them as a mother

> pleads with her boy that he will not grieve her, or as a fond sister entreats a brother to return to their father's home and seek reconciliation: argument must be quickened into persuasion by the living warmth of love. Cold logic has its force, but when made red-hot with affection, the power of tender argument is inconceivable.... When passionate zeal has carried the man himself away his speech becomes an irresistible torrent, sweeping all before it. A man known to be godly and devout, and felt to be large-hearted and self-sacrificing, has a power in his very person ... but when he comes to plead and persuade, even to tears, his influence is wonderful and God the Holy Spirit yokes it into His service. Brethren, we must plead. Entreaties and beseechings must blend with instructions.

The evangelist, though, is more than just a preacher. Effective evangelism can be done by those who would never deliver a sermon in a pulpit. There are fine evangelists working one-to-one in a community, perhaps targeting a particular group of people, who find God taking hold of their words to use them in the saving of souls.

This work is dangerous in that it is open to abuse, but if the evangelist is dependent upon God, he will not be guilty of excesses. We need evangelists who honour God in their lives, in their ministry, their earnest desire for fruit, and in the increase which God gives.

2. CHURCHES SHOULD LOOK FOR EVANGELISTS

If God 'gave ... some evangelists', they must be in our congregations and churches. Perhaps we could help identify and encourage them.

I have read many definitions of evangelism, some profound and some verbose. However, as far as I understand it, evangelism is preaching the gospel to non-Christians who are listening.

From that definition, we see that evangelism is not just proclaiming with the thought that God can use anything to touch and convert people. Of course, there is some truth in that, but true evangelism should have a standard of excellence in its content and presentation. This does not undermine our total dependence upon the Lord to bless, and indeed to over-rule the many unexpected occurrences and mistakes that constantly remind us of our inadequacy!

On the other hand, evangelism is not simply preaching the gospel. There have to be unsaved people present to hear the gospel. Prior to some evangelistic meetings, I have been met with the words: 'There are no unconverted here, but preach the gospel anyway, you don't know what might happen!' Pews, pillars and portraits do not get converted and therefore cannot be evangelized! However, it is dangerous to assume that congregations are all comprised of saved people.

Neither can we call preaching the gospel to non-Christians evangelism, if they are not listening. To shout out messages to passing crowds who do not stop to listen or talk is not evangelism. (Having said that, I recall that I was once sent a postcard, bought in a tourist shop in Bermuda, of Johnny Barnes, a local man who is well known for having stood for years at Crow Lane roundabout winsomely telling all who pass by that God loves them!) However, it is possible to present a reasoned and convincing argument for Christianity in a way that is both commending to the gospel and also attracting the attention of the crowds. Unless we are wise, street preaching will do more harm than good, and will serve only as a sop to the conscience of those who really ought to be proclaiming Christ more effectively. They will feel that they are 'doing their bit'. Having said that, however, I am convinced that every preacher ought to preach in the open-air, just as they ought to try and write gospel tracts. One trusts that it will be a blessing to those who listen to the message or receive the literature; but it will certainly be helpful to the evangelist for it will teach him or her again about the attitudes and reactions of ordinary, unsaved people.

Evangelism, then, is proclaiming the gospel to non-Christians who are listening. Evangelists are to be godly and evangelical, gifted and called by God to proclaim to the lost world the gospel of the Lord Jesus. They are a vital part of the work of reaching the world for Christ. The evangelist is a messenger and herald of the Good News.

Surely there must be such people within our churches, youth fellowships and Christian Unions, who know what they believe and want above all else to herald to all the historic Christian message of the finished work of Christ. It cannot be that burdened people are a thing of a bygone Christian era. Perhaps we are failing to look for such people.

Christian leaders, especially, ought to be on the look out for people with evangelistic energy, burden and talent, and encourage them to develop their gift. This can be done by prayer, verbal encouragement and the creation of ministry opportunities for these up-and-coming evangelists. I clearly remember the place, the time and the man who first said to me that he thought God had given me the gift of the evangelist. There was no cause for boasting, for what have we that we have not received (1 Cor. 4:6-7)? However, it was the first indication of what God had in store for me, and that in itself was a great encouragement, especially since it had come from someone whose judgment I trusted.

3. CHURCHES SHOULD TRAIN EVANGELISTS

Evangelists are more 'caught than taught'. In other words, there are people who have a gift from God for the work of evangelism, who have been challenged by example and constrained by the Word and the Holy Spirit. However, every gift needs to be developed and refined. It is therefore a relevant question to ask what training opportunities exist for would-be evangelists? Often young people with evangelistic hearts go to Bible College, but there is a tendency for their fervour to be quenched by the demands of the discipline of learning, and the pursuit of academic success, especially if there is not a constant programme of evangelism incorporated within the training programme. In other places the burden and gift is redirected toward Bible teaching or pastoral work. We do need Bible teachers and pastors, but if that is not the work to which God has called the person, he will never experience true joy in working for God, nor be as strategic in the Lord's service as he might otherwise have been.

One of the great values of open-air meetings or street preaching or short-term missions, and so on, is that they give the opportunity for young people to be trained and improve their gift through exercising it. Speaking personally, most of my early preaching was done on street corners, beaches, promenades or pedestrian precincts, and I still like to be involved in this work. It provides a way to reach total outsiders (especially men) with the gospel, and it also creates a regular opportunity for young people to start to learn to share their testimony, then give a gospel talk, albeit in the rather ruthless setting of not having a patient, tolerant, captive audience. Every preacher ought to go into the open air to preach. They will find it a great classroom, and the work itself a teacher of good communication. Catching the attention of a crowd in the open air and putting across Bible truths in that context may be worth more than many a certificate of credit in homiletics – though the two are not mutually exclusive! In his *Lectures to My Students*, Spurgeon traces this work back to Enoch, Noah, Moses, Joshua, Samuel, Elijah, Jonah, Nehemiah, Ezra, Peter and Paul, as well as the Lord

99

Himself! The open air was the cathedral site for Wesley and Whitefield as well as Christmas Evans of Wales, the Haldanes in Scotland, Rowland Hill in England and Peter Cartwright, Lorenzo Dow and many others in the USA.

For forty-three years Robert Flockhart of Edinburgh preached every evening, in all weathers, often with the backcloth of great opposition from the police, Unitarians and Roman Catholics. As an old man he said, 'Compassion to the souls of men drove me to the streets and lanes of my native city to plead with sinners and persuade them to come to Jesus. The love of Christ constrained me.'

Those involved with evangelistic endeavour might invite young people to shadow them in special events, or with a carefully chosen person, for an extended period of time. This principle is illustrated in the Old Testament by King Saul who 'when [he] saw any strong man or any valiant man, he took him for himself' (1 Sam. 14:52). This must be one of the few respects in which King Saul is a good example to follow! The idea is taught in the New Testament by the examples of the Lord Jesus and the apostle Paul, who, writing to Timothy, spoke of four generations of Christians: 'And the things that you have heard from me among many witnesses, commit these to faithful men who will be able to teach others also' (2 Tim. 2:2). As D. L. Moody said, 'You can do the work of ten men, or teach ten men to do it.'

The task of worldwide evangelism is so vast that we must enlist as many people as possible in this work. 'I scarcely know of any greater blessing to the church than the sending forth of earnest, indefatigable, anointed men of God, taught of the Lord to be winners of souls,' says Paul Bassett, in his book about evangelism, *God's Way*.

But, there has to be a consistently high standard of holiness, sacrifice and commitment. In a letter to Alexander Mather, one of his most trusted preachers, John Wesley regretted that many of the preachers were not 'alive to God' and were fearful of shame, toil and hardship. He added: 'Give me one hundred preachers who fear nothing but sin and desire nothing but God, and I care not a straw whether they be clergymen or laymen, such alone will shake the gates of hell and set up the kingdom of heaven upon earth.' Death to self, and life in and for Christ is the pre-requisite of anyone who is going to live a life which will count for eternity.

4. CHURCHES SHOULD USE EVANGELISTS

The godless society around us has intimidated Christians into near silence. Instead of becoming more lovingly aggressive in our evangelism, we seem to have huddled ourselves into safe zones, or redirected our efforts into social or political action. The finest act of friendship and the greatest social good we can do is to preach the gospel to unconverted people. What a transformation takes place when an individual, in repentance and faith, trusts Christ! Christ makes the drunkard, sober; the immoral, pure; the dishonest, trustworthy; the selfish, selfless; the godless, godly. This is not to say that Christians should not be involved in seeking to alleviate social ills, but our priority has to be to win souls for Christ and eternity.

I wish that every church was regularly holding evangelistic events and missions. Let us remember that '... even if our gospel is veiled, it is veiled to those that are perishing' (2 Cor. 4:3). It appears that, as in the days of Amos, there is a famine in the land, not of bread, nor of water, but of hearing the words of the Lord (Amos 8:11). Isaiah says that just as the land needs to be covered with rain and snow, so it needs to be saturated with the Word of God (Isa. 55:10-11). The Word should be getting out everywhere – through posters, tracts, Gospels, preaching, on radio and television, in churches and in the open. There is ample opportunity; we are the ones to take it. Like rain and snow, at first it may appear that the Word is falling and being wasted, but let the fall be constant and heavy, it will have its effect and cover the land.

Evangelists should be used to spearhead the evangelistic strategy of groups and individuals. Talking to young pastors C. H. Spurgeon said:

> To call in another brother every now and then to take the lead in evangelistic service will be found very wise and useful; for there are some fish that will never be taken in your net, but will surely fall to the lot of another fisherman. Fresh voices penetrate where the accustomed sound has lost effect, and they tend also to beget a deeper interest in those already attentive. Sound and prudent evangelists may lend help even to the most efficient pastor, and gather in fruit which he has failed to reach; at any rate it makes a break in the continuity of ordinary services, and renders them less likely to become monotonous. Never suffer jealousy to hinder you in this. Suppose another lamp should outshine yours, what will it matter so long as it brings light to those whose welfare you are seeking? Say with Moses, 'Would to God all the Lord's servants were prophets.' He who is free from selfish jealousy will find that no occasion will suggest it; his people may be well aware that their pastor is excelled by others in talent, but they will be ready to assert that he is surpassed by none in love to their souls. It is not needful for a loving son to believe that his father is the most learned man in the parish; he loves him for his own sake, and not because he is superior to others. Call in every now and then a warm-hearted neighbour, utilise the talent in the church itself, and procure the services of some eminent soul-winner, and this may, in God's hand, break up the hard soil for you, and bring you brighter days.

Others have suggested innumerable alternative ideas for events that may be used evangelistically, I have found that the Lord still uses, above everything else, the 'foolishness of preaching'

(1 Cor. 1:20–2:2) to win people to Christ. Other events may bring in more unconverted people, but these occasions are less likely to be reaping opportunities. The people who can arrange effective evangelistic meetings are, to my mind, the salt of the earth. Unconverted people who come to evangelistic meetings are usually people who are brought (not just invited). If there is confidence in the evangelist, and the programme of the event, Christians will bring their friends for whom they have been praying and witnessing, and often God uses such events in a mighty way. Generally, the ones converted are those who have been brought and prayed for.

It is possible to create an evangelistic programme which does not assume that the unconverted friend is familiar with Christian worship. Without imposing our Christian traditions on invited guests, a programme around a theme incorporating musicians, a testimony, video clip and culminating in the preaching of the Word can be very effective. In smaller halls, rather than seating people in pews or rows, it is more relaxed to arrange chairs around coffee tables with light refreshments for them to nibble throughout. I have not found that this distracts from the gospel at all.

We are commanded to go into the world and preach the gospel to every creature (Mark 16:15; Col. 1:23), and Peter says that we should 'always be ready to give a defense to everyone who asks you a reason for the hope that is in you, with meekness and fear' (1 Pet. 3:15). 'Everyone' includes those from each colour, culture, continent and country, regardless of their economic status. Neither rags nor riches, mansions nor mud huts, intellect nor lack of it rid people of a sinful heart and their need for salvation.

5. Churches should pray for evangelists

Evangelists are to be prayerful people. They are to seek God's blessing on their ministry and the people they are ministering to. Hudson Taylor could say after forty years of evangelism in China, 'Over the past forty years, the sun has never risen in China without finding me on my knees praying.' But, evangelists, like others, have their weaknesses and need prayer (more on this in Chapter 14). We need to be in fervent prayer for the people listening, and for the ministry. God will and does use his servants, but we move forward only in dependence upon him. The work of saving souls is the Lord's work. We can and should organize and preach, but are unable to convert any individual. As the apostle Paul said: 'I planted, Apollos watered, but God gave the increase. So then neither he who plants is anything, nor he who waters, but God who gives the increase' (1 Cor. 3:6-7). God works in answer to prayer and obedience, for His glory.

The importance of evangelism can be emphasised in a fellowship or church by regularly asking for prayer concerning people who have been witnessed to, or about whom the fellowship is burdened. Also praying specifically for unsaved people by name, following their progress and showing concern helps keep evangelism high on the agenda of the church.

Regular prayers in church and prayer meetings lift the importance of evangelistic work in the minds of believers, as well as being a blessing in themselves. What an encouragement it is for evangelists to know that they are being prayed for, indeed to know that people are receiving, reading and regularly using the prayer letters which are sent out. The evangelist is not necessarily the key figure, but needs many others to keep him in the position to be able to do the work effectively. The evangelist needs prayer supporters. All Christians (including the housebound and those who feel they can do little for the Lord) can be involved in evangelization by their prayers. Evangelists have a duty to keep their prayer-partners well informed of needs and opportunities.

The apostle Paul set an example of this: writing to the Corinthians he said, 'For a great and effective door has opened to me and there are many adversaries' (1 Cor. 16:9). To the Colossians he said, 'Continue earnestly in prayer, being vigilant in it with thanksgiving; meanwhile praying also for us that God would open to us a door for the word, to speak the mystery of Christ, for which I am also in chains, that I may make it manifest, as I ought to speak' (4:2-4). Every evangelist covets the prayers of others, and will pray that his own heart will be kept in tune with the Lord's heart and love for the lost (Matt. 9:36-38).

> Dear Lord, I ask for the eyes that see
> Deep down to the world's sore need,
> I ask for a love that holds not back,
> But pours out itself indeed;
> I want the passionate power of prayer,
> That yearns for the great crowd's soul,
> I want to go 'mong the fainting sheep
> And tell them my Lord makes whole.
>
> Let me look at the crowd as my Saviour did,
> Till my eyes with tears grow dim;
> Let me look till I pity the wandering sheep,
> And love them for love of Him.
>
> W. Gardiner-Hunter

6. Churches should support evangelists

Missionaries and evangelists need support. For myself, I never find it easy to talk about financial matters. Is it pride, culture or a genuine relying on the Lord to provide funds and meet needs? In this and other areas evangelists should be accountable to people who are friendly and firm enough to be able to ask awkward questions from a loving heart. We all need checks and balances. For myself, I, and the Association of Evangelists with whom

I am connected, do not ask for or solicit funds. Prayer letters are what they claim to be; they are not begging letters. However, there are different ways of operating, and each evangelist has to give account to God as to how he has raised and used his funds. To support financially or in other practical ways is a means of being part of the work of evangelism that is being done through the evangelist. It is a great encouragement to know of individuals and churches who are really behind an evangelist. A gift not only 'supports' the evangelist financially but demonstrates a greater support, which is worth more than gold.

These then are some ways in which churches can be involved to encourage and promote the work of evangelism and seek to remedy the desperate plight of men and women facing a lost eternity.

11 The Bible as a tool

God's heart is that of a true evangelist – His earnest desire is that none should perish (2 Pet. 3:9). To that end He has revealed Himself to a lost world. The two basic means of his revelation are the living and loving Word, namely Christ; and also the written Word, which is the Bible. We have already considered Christ as an evangelist, but there is a sense in which the Bible is also an evangelist. Admittedly, the Bible does not have personality, and evangelists are people. Nevertheless the Bible has been the means of countless numbers coming to faith in Christ. God delights to use his Word. It is the most basic and finest tool for the evangelist.

EVANGELISTIC POWER
The Bible has found its way into the hearts and homes of people who would never have entertained a human evangelist. The

evangelistic power of the Bible is stated repeatedly in its own pages: 'The law of the LORD is perfect, converting the soul' (Ps. 19:7); 'I will never forget Your precepts, for by them You have given me life' (Ps. 119:93); 'So then faith comes by hearing, and hearing by the word of God' (Rom. 10:17), and so on. (See also John 20:31; Eph. 6:17; 2 Tim. 3:16.)

In Jesus' parable of the sower and the seed, the seed is the Word of God (Mark 4:14), and therefore is to be scattered, for when it falls on good ground it will result in much fruit. The measure of a preacher today and a prophet of old is in their ability to proclaim the Word of God. Jokes and illustrations bring light relief and illuminate truths, but only the Word of God has the intrinsic power to touch lives and save souls. It is not only the authority of those who stand to speak for Christ, but it is the basis of all their work. Billy Graham's oft-repeated phrase, 'The Bible says...' has become almost legendary and is a credit to him. As a younger preacher, he would always ensure that there were at least twenty-five Bible texts in each message, believing that God uses His Word to touch the lives of people! It would be impossible to prove, but it is quite conceivable that more people have been converted through the straightforward reading of the Bible than through any human evangelist.

One such person was Aurelius Augustinus, Professor of Rhetoric at Milan. In the summer of 380 he sat weeping in the garden of his friend Alypius. He had lived the life of a prodigal and, though he wanted to change, he felt powerless to overcome his old life and start a new one. As he sat, he heard a child singing in a neighbouring house, 'Take up and read! Take up and read!' He picked up the scroll which lay at his friend's side and read, 'not in revelry and drunkenness, not in licentiousness and lewdness, not in strife and envy; but put on the Lord

Jesus Christ, and make no provision for the flesh, to fulfil its lusts' (Rom. 13:13b-14). He explained his thoughts: 'No further would I read, nor had I any need; instantly, at the end of this sentence, a clear light flooded my heart and all the darkness of doubt vanished away.' God spoke through the most appropriate Bible text for a man who had thrown himself into a life of godlessness, and saved a soul to whom the church and the world are indebted.

Twelve centuries later in November 1515, Martin Luther, lawyer, monk and Professor of Sacred Theology in the University of Wittenberg, began to expound the same Bible book, Paul's letter to the Romans, and came to appreciate the doctrine of justification by faith. He began to wrestle with and grapple to understand the phrase, 'the righteousness of God'; but this led him to grasp the gospel, and later he was to describe how that passage 'became to me the gateway to heaven'. Of course, it was Luther's exposition of this that led to John Wesley's conversion on 24 May 1738.

Warren Nelson's biography of T. C. Hammond tells an extraordinary story: Thomas Connellan was ordained as Roman Catholic priest in Southern Ireland in 1882 and worked on the staff of the cathedral in Athlone. However, his own study of the Bible led him seriously to doubt his church's doctrine of transubstantiation (the teaching that in the mass the bread and wine become the body and blood of Christ). This became such a crisis of mind for him that he made a dramatic departure by pretending he had drowned in the River Shannon near Athlone. The townspeople fell for it and the newspapers were filled with warm tributes to his Catholic piety and other virtues. Connellan, however, travelled to London, and found his way to St. Paul's Church, Onslow Square, where the Rev. M. R. Webb-Peploe had the joy of leading him into the full light of the gospel.

Some time later, Connellan became convinced that he should return to Ireland to declare his faith and his reasons for leaving the Roman Catholic Church. He was attacked by a crowd in Athlone and later excommunicated by his church. However, when his character was vilified, his friends only needed to produce the glowing newspaper accounts of his life as a priest to silence the critics. In 1890 he was licensed as a clergyman by the Church of Ireland. He set up the Connellan Mission, and began a monthly evangelical paper called *The Catholic* which he edited until his death.

Decision magazine of March 1984 tells the story of Jeff Robinson, a Yorkshire miner, brought up in a large, non-Christian family. Travelling on the top deck of a double-decker bus, he was fiddling with his bus ticket when he noticed that printed on the back of it was the first part of John 3:16, 'For God so loved the world that He gave His only begotten Son...' The next part of the verse was on the next ticket! The verse so spoke to him, that he went back home, took down the Bible he had been given at school and began to read. Then he went with his girlfriend to church where they were both converted!

John Nicholson, Samuel Hill and W. J. Knights, aware of the power of the Bible to touch people's lives, started the Gideons, an association of Christians in business who distribute Bibles and New Testaments by the million to individuals and public places. They have thousands of amazing stories of how the Lord uses these worldwide.

The earth is the Lord's and has a basic need to be covered with the Word of God.

> For as the rain comes down,
>> and the snow from heaven,
> And do not return there,
>> But water the earth,

And make it bring forth and bud,
     That it may give seed to the sower
          And bread to the eater,
So shall My word be that goes forth from My mouth;
     It shall not return to me void,
But it shall accomplish what I please,
     And it shall prosper in the thing for which I sent it. (Isa. 55:10-11)

It does my heart good to see the Word of God on posters, noticeboards and greeting cards. If nothing else this practice provides a backcloth for the times when the gospel is preached. The Lord can use the printed word to bring people to faith in ways we would never dream possible. Distribution of the Scripture is, in effect, scattering evangelists here and there. Who knows when these messages themselves will be used to win someone to Christ?

12 The tract as a tool

Vincent Taylor maintained that the test of any theologian is whether he can write a tract!

Standing at a stall in a missionary exhibition of a large Christian conference, I experienced a sense of disappointment as time after time Christians said, 'Oh, we used to give away tracts, but it is years since we last did.' In a time when there is great spiritual ignorance, and we are looking for ways to open conversations of consequence, let me write in praise of the humble tract!

I do not know of any easier way to share the good news of Jesus Christ than through a short, simple leaflet which fits into my wallet, pocket or bag and is an abiding message ready to go to work and be used of God at any time.

Tracts are the key to open the door of conversation, and then they are a reminder of what the message just shared is all about.

It is a self-imposed 'rule' of my life never to go anywhere without tracts, and wherever possible I seek to pass them on to people I happen to meet.

How else could I get into conversation with the person in the garage, if I did not have a tract? As I take my receipt, it is easy to hand back a tract with the words, 'May I give you a little gospel leaflet?' Then, looking the person in the eye, I add, 'It simply explains how Christ Jesus came into the world to save sinners... and I'm sure you would agree, we qualify!' If the reaction is one of seeming interest, I might ask, 'Have you ever given serious thought to Jesus Christ?'

Personal evangelism can be tough at times, but if it is one-to-one, rather than within a group, done with a reassuring smile and a confidence in Christ, it can be a thrilling, daily ministry. As an evangelist, I believe that street work is vital for me. I trust it is a blessing to the people I meet, but they are a real blessing to me. They help me not to grow out of touch with ordinary, unsaved people. Even their apathy or antagonism can minister to me, in that it reminds me where people are in their attitudes to the Lord.

Success in witnessing is simply speaking of Christ in the power of the Holy Spirit and leaving the results to God. The tract can be the way to turn the direction of small talk to conversation concerning Christ and can be given away anywhere – in restaurants, shops, on the train or bus or plane, in a queue, to the postman or door-to-door salesman. It may not always be possible to talk with a particular person, but who knows how the Lord might use the printed word as an evangelist, if passed on prayerfully? (Isa. 55:11).

Undoubtedly, many tracts will be discarded, but in days of spiritual ignorance, it is something for which to be grateful if at least some are read. The evangelist can be an example to others in this matter. Enthusiasm is infectious, and when Christians see a spiritual leader with a burden to be constantly about the Master's business, it makes its impact. A university student told me how deeply impressed he had been by the British preacher, Leith Samuel. They were travelling on the same train, and Mr Samuel had approached every passenger offering them a free copy of his *Answer to ...* booklet to read on their journey. There is joy in the heart of every Christian who tells someone of their need for repentance and faith.

Every so often it is good to organize a mass distribution of tracts in a locality; in the shopping centre, the park or at sporting events. George Muller used to give out tracts at public executions! Today we have people 'hanging around' in other places! Many will not have read an attractive Christian leaflet until we meet them. You may be a challenging encouragement to fellow Christians and would-be evangelists as you take a group of volunteers to help in the task.

Tracts know no geographical or political borders. There are Christians regularly sending gospel literature through the mail to otherwise 'closed' countries. Also, for those who live near a seaport or airport or some kind of tourist centre, it is possible to reach people from all over the world. The range of nationalities passing through London, for example, is astounding. These people may have had no previous contact with Christians but may be glad to accept and read a tract offered to them.

Tracts can also be placed in letters of all kinds – when paying bills, or writing to friends or businesses, sending greeting cards or writing to people who have been absent from church for a while. The fact is, many people who would never attend church or read the Bible will read a tract – and in doing so will receive the Word of God. My attitude to junk mail has been transformed by tracts. I used to be irritated by the thirty-second waste of life each unsolicited letter caused. Now I relish opening such mail because of the enclosed pre-paid envelope. They want to hear from me, so enclosing a tract, I do not disappoint them!

There are tracts for every occasion, every need and every type of person. They can be distributed by anybody, regardless of age, sex, race or education, but the evangelist should set the lead in this. Children especially treasure something which is attractive and will often re-read something they like several times. A supply of foreign-language tracts makes it possible to reach people who could not otherwise be spoken to about Christ.

This is not just theory. As a tract writer, publisher and distributor, I can testify to the fact that I frequently receive letters from people who have been converted by this means. Sometimes the tract has been given to them; sometimes it has been found on a train, in an airport lounge, telephone kiosk or the like. They come from every walk of life, from all over the country, and indeed, the world. The Bible promises: 'He who sows sparingly will also reap sparingly, and he who sows bountifully will also reap bountifully' (2 Cor. 9:6).

A tract may be an inanimate evangelist, but it can be used of God to bring life where once there was death. Hudson Taylor, the founder of the China Inland Mission, was converted through reading a tract when he was just seventeen years of age. Dave Burke, Christian author and pastor, was converted to Christ through reading a gospel left under the windscreen wiper of his car when holidaying in Europe. Mehdi Dibaj, an Iranian Moslem, turned to Christ after reading a tract. He was martyred for his faith in 1994 in Iran after living a life of bold proclamation of the gospel in that Islamic land.

We do not know how the Lord will use another gospel tract, but for some, the gospel leaflet may be the only 'evangelist' they will ever meet.

E-VANGELISM

When the Great Commission was given to the disciples, the only means of transport was on donkey or unreliable sailing vessels, as the apostle Paul found to his cost! Now we have planes, trains and cars – and can communicate via radio, telephone, television and electronic mail. The big, big world has become quite small.

Now, thanks to the internet our earth is even smaller. Living in a global village provides exciting new and innovative ways to make Christ known. As Mark Moring writes in *Christianity on Line* (November – December, 1999), 'Jesus might have had the whole world in His hands, but we have got it right at our fingertips.' The Net gives Christians a means of reaching millions of people at a time, and many can be from areas that are virtually unreachable through more traditional means.

There is scope for both large Christian organisations to create evangelistic or devotional web sites, as well as for the lone Christian to chat on line. (Back to the Bible Broadcasts say that 150 are coming to salvation each month through their work on the internet, and that they are receiving around 4.7 million hits per month.) Attractive web sites are not enough though. There needs to be marketing and promotion of the site to bring in 'the seekers'. Proclaiming Christ in cyberspace is much the same as sharing Him anywhere else. The gospel remains the same, and the need just as urgent. Some preachers can be heard on line and therefore have the potential to reach millions.

There is also opportunity for the less well known to use E-vangelism. There can be 'cyber street corner evangelists' (as Moring calls them). Through chat rooms it is possible to communicate with people all over the world. Inevitably there are dangers – time can be wasted and often the subjects discussed are unhelpful. Nevertheless, there is surely a God-given opportunity to redeem the chat by talking about the Lord. This is a ministry open to young and old alike who are on line. Gerald Boyd is an 82 year old retired pastor who runs an evangelistic site and 'works the chat rooms about five hours a day'. He says, 'The technology makes it possible for me to strike up a conversation with a housewife in Toronto, a teen Satanist in Germany, an atheist in New York and a seeker in London. I have never had this kind of opportunity to interact with such a variety of people, all within the reach of my fingertips.'

A young evangelist is in regular discussion with people living in countries that would normally be inaccessible to missionaries. I think in years to come we will see a growth in the use of electronic mail in reaching people for Christ, but I am still convinced that eye ball to eye ball evangelism must never be lost.

13 The children's evangelist

'When I approach a child, he inspires in me two sentiments: tenderness, for what he is, and respect for what he may become'. (Louis Pasteur)

What do Polycarp, Matthew Henry, Richard Baxter, Jonathan Edwards, Mary Slessor, Lord Shaftesbury, Amy Carmichael and Jim Elliott have in common? They were all converted as children.

Perhaps you trusted Christ when you were very young. After all, children are people, they do have souls! When the Lord of all glory clothed himself in human flesh, He did not become an adult straight away, instead He became a baby and then a child. Christ fully identified Himself with humanity. 'He is our childhood's pattern,' says the Christmas carol, but He is also the adult pattern of a right attitude to children.

Without manipulating or abusing a child's innocent trust, it is part of the adult privilege to point little ones in the direction of the Lord. The children's evangelist will be a specialist in this, developing his or her own expertise under God.

A DUTY AND A PRIVILEGE

It seems that fewer churches have a children's talk in their morning services, even though this used to be so effective in teaching young and old alike! The Bible, however, makes clear our duty to instruct children. Psalm 34:11 says, 'Come, you children, listen to me; I will teach you the fear of the LORD.' Joel 1:3 urges God's people to pass on the words and works of God: 'Tell your children about it, let your children tell their children, and their children another generation.'

The Lord God Himself (Exod. 20:12), Moses (Deut. 31:12), Joshua (Josh. 8:35), David (Ps. 34:11), Solomon (Eccles. 12:1) and the Lord Jesus (Matt. 19:14) all taught and instructed children concerning the Word of God. We learn in the Bible of children listening to the Scriptures (Josh. 8:35), rejoicing in the Lord (Neh. 12:43), giving to God (John 6:9), as well as praising the Lord Jesus (Matt. 21:15).

Children are often so open to the straightforward truths of the gospel. When the Holy Spirit speaks, they will readily respond to the claims of Christ on their young lives. They willingly acknowledge that they have done bad things and have sinned. They do trust that the Lord Jesus loves them so much that he died for them. They can be sorry for sin and, knowing that the Lord loves them, respond in love to Him. They want to belong to His family.

There has been a tendency in 'hands-on' children's work to move away from teaching children to memorize Scripture. Such an approach is hardly biblical and not helpful in giving little ones the weapons with which to defeat Satan and build their own faith.

Who knows what God may do with a young Christian? The duty of the children's evangelist is not to indoctrinate, but to teach the things of God and to bring children to Christ. Hudson

Pope, a great children's evangelist, said of them, 'If they have never heard the gospel before, they will hear it tonight,' and to other evangelists he said, 'You may speak to half a dozen children in an evening, but will you remember this? While the fifth one is number five to you, he himself is not one of a number. To him, it is the crisis of his life.... To each one of the six it may be their supreme moment, so never get used to doing children's work.'

THE IMPORTANCE OF CHILDREN'S WORK

Children's work on a village green, in a church or home, Good News Club, on a beach, in school or Sunday School, club or uniformed movement is never easy. Too often the church has been guilty of palming off Sunday school classes to the spiritually weak and emotionally immature, rather than treat the work of investing truth in young, receptive hearts, as a serious spiritual work. Similarly, there is a tendency to think that a children's evangelist is second best, or for those who do not know deep theology. But those who feel this must be forgetting that those who teach simply, must know deeply. As evangelists, we should never be guilty of feeling that children's work is beneath us, even if it is not the major task in our lives. We should do our utmost to encourage evangelists involved in children's evangelism.

Hudson Pope often said in later life, 'It sometimes takes a whole mission to save one child. I notice, looking back over the years, how often each mission is the out-bringing of one person who goes on and does exploits. I do not mean that others do not stand, but often there is one who outstands, and it looks as though God allowed a great effort in order to win one – joy in the presence of the angels over one.' And C. H. Spurgeon said, 'I have more confidence in the spiritual life of the children

I have received into this church, than I have in the adults.' History testifies to the heartwarming fact that a youngster can be truly converted and kept for great usefulness.

Polycarp, just before his martyrdom at the age of 95 said, 'For eighty and six years I have served my King and He has done for me no harm', thereby declaring that he had been converted at the age of nine. Matthew Henry, the Bible commentator, was brought to Christ when he was eleven. The great pastor, Richard Baxter, was converted at the age of six. Robert Moffat, the missionary, was only a young boy; Helen Cadbury, the founder of the Pocket Testament League, was twelve; missionary Rosalind Goforth was eleven and the Countess of Huntingdon and Isaac Watts only nine. All Catherine Booth's eight children had been led to Christ before they were ten years old. J. C. Ryle, the first Bishop of Liverpool, said the happiest little girl he ever knew was a Christian, although only eight years old and blind. Jonathan Edwards and Mary Slessor were converted at seven; Amy Carmichael at nine whilst at boarding school, and Jim Elliot at six. Before sin leaves its scars, which although they may be forgiven, permanently mar the earthly life of people, may we seek to bring youngsters to new birth.

Churches and organizations such as Child Evangelism Fellowship, Awana, Scripture Union and United Beach Missions in Europe have found that because they have shown genuine interest in children, parents have been willing to attend adult and family evangelistic activities. This has brought blessing to the whole family. Christian parents obviously are the best means of reaching children, but a converted child can pave the way towards reaching the unconverted parents. We should not despise youngsters who put their faith in Christ. To quote Hudson Pope again , 'Never underrate the under eights!'

'SUFFER THE LITTLE CHILDREN'

The world is rightly alarmed by the increase in child abuse. Children have often been the victims of the selfish and sinful. Abuse is nothing new. For centuries children have been sacrificed (Jer. 32:35) and slaughtered (Matt. 2:16). The psalmist described the situation with words which are equally appropriate for today: 'They even sacrificed their sons and daughters to demons, and shed innocent blood, even the blood of their sons and daughters whom they sacrificed to the idols of Canaan, and the land was polluted with blood' (Ps. 106:36-38).

I wonder whether, despite all the fine children's visual aids and helps, we sometimes adopt the same wrongful attitudes as Christ's disciples:

> When mothers of Salem
> Their children brought to Jesus
> The stern disciples drove them back
> And bid them all depart:
> But Jesus saw them ere they fled
> And sweetly smiled and kindly said,
> 'Suffer little children to come unto Me.'

Jesus warned against despising any of His little ones (Matt. 18:6-10). We can be guilty of this by plain nastiness or simple neglect. Not everyone is called to be a children's evangelist, but all are commanded to be kind, caring and concerned towards the vulnerable.

Children know and love the person who shows interest in them. I will never forget the old man who gave a sweet to every child after the Sunday service as they shook hands with the preacher. Similarly, a genial person who talks to the children who live in the neighbourhood will be remembered fondly. Evangelists, including children's evangelists, need to be accessible. The Lord was always so. The children ran to Him and flocked about Him.

CHILDREN TEACH US

Our attitude to children will reveal our true character and our attitude to Christ. A Roman Catholic man was converted to Christ through John Wesley. It was nothing to do with what Wesley said, but simply that the man was deeply impressed by the way Wesley bent down and kissed a small child who stood by the steps from which John Wesley was preaching. John Newton, the converted slave trader and ship's captain, showed his true character as he frequently gathered around him boys, and told them seafaring tales and Bible stories. And John Updike observed: 'If men do not keep on speaking terms with children, they cease to be men and become merely machines for eating, and earning money.'

We read of the New Jerusalem that 'the streets of the city shall be full of boys and girls playing in the streets' (Zech. 8:5). God is concerned for children: 'He will feed His flock like a shepherd; He will gather the lambs with His arm, and carry them in His bosom and gently lead those who are with young' (Isa. 40:11). He even sends guardian angels to look after them (Matt. 18:10). Shouldn't we, in like manner, show compassion and evangelistic concern for children? This can be done in a number of ways.

We should pray for children (Ezra 8:21). We should pray that they may live protected from evil influences, circumstances and people, and that they may grow to trust, love and serve the Saviour of sinners who bled, died and rose again for them. By praying for children for whom no-one else prays there can be great service done – making the un-prayed-for-child a prayed-for-child! 'For this child I prayed, and the LORD has granted me my petition which I asked of Him' (1 Sam. 1:27).

We should love children (Mark 10:16). If their noise irritates us, perhaps it is our sanctification that should be questioned, rather then theirs! To evangelize them is one of the most loving things we can do for children.

We should teach children (Deut. 31:12). There is to be systematic Bible teaching where possible, but the evangelistic thrust for children can be very blessed indeed. The evangelist will be careful not to abuse the child's basic desire to please adults, which may include the child even praying a prayer of response but without conviction or real faith.

We should write to them. Children delight to receive letters, often keeping them and reading them many times over. Therefore, there is great value in sowing little seeds of truth through letters.

We should take time with children. Few children are really listened to or talked with. Jesus sat them on His knee. We should make ourselves approachable by approaching them and spending time with them.

Children's evangelism is a high and holy calling. Let us not despise these little ones, or their evangelists.

14 The message and messenger

Imagine a man walking along a cliff edge who suddenly sees, to his horror, a person drowning in the sea, the waves beating his helpless body against the rocks. Immediately a leisurely afternoon stroll is transformed into a dramatic act of rescue, as the first man rips off his coat and dives into the sea. There follows a desperate struggle to save the drowning man. At last, the rescued man staggers from the sea, with only cuts and bruises to show for his ordeal, but the rescuer has been very seriously injured, with many broken bones. A helicopter takes him to hospital where he spends days in intensive care, followed by the prospect of a lengthy recovery period.

Some weeks later the rescued man goes to visit his saviour. They talk for a while, and the rescuer offers his visitor a sugar-coated mint. Walking away from the hospital, the rescued man meets a friend who asks him where he has been. He is reluctant to say, but when pressed, he replies, 'I've been to see a friend who gave me a sugar-coated mint.'

There is something wrong with that reply. After all, the man owes his very life to the other person who is left slowly recovering in hospital. What is a sugar-coated mint compared with the fact that the man almost lost his life to save him?

There is a danger in evangelistic preaching that the emphasis is on the additional blessings that come as a result of Christian conversion, rather than the basic facts that Christ suffered, died and rose again for our justification (1 Cor. 15:1-4). To speak of joy, healing, love, purpose, and so on, is to speak of the sugar-coated mint, but Christ has done something far more wonderful and eternal in our lives. Dr William Sangster said, 'When we preach the gospel, we are not offering full life instead of scant life, but life instead of death.' Our standing before the Lord has been radically altered through His grace. When preaching and emphasizing the joy in salvation, there is an option – an individual can get 'joy' in pubs and clubs or through drugs and alcohol. But when emphasizing the need to get right with God, there is no option, for only Christ can give that relationship. The Welsh evangelist David Shepherd says, 'It is more important to be right than happy, but I am never so happy as when I am right.' As the world speaks of tinsel and trees at Christmas but often misses the real significance of the incarnation, so evangelists can be in danger of missing the hub of the gospel upon which all true Christianity turns.

The evangelist has the most wonderful message in the world. God sent Peter, not an angel, to Cornelius, and He still sends people to convey his message to men and women. It is the message which comes from the heart of heaven to the hearts of men and women. It meets our deepest needs by exposing our sin, and then pointing us away from ourselves to Christ Himself. Evangelists will teach that sin is the most expensive thing in the world. Whether forgiven or not, sin's cost is infinite. Pardoned, the cost falls chiefly on Christ, the Substitute for sin and sinners; unpardoned, it must fall on the guilty sinner, and has eternal consequences. People must realize their dreadful position before God, before they will turn to Him for salvation. Inadvertently, the woman of Tekoa focused on the significance of our gospel when she said to King David: 'For we will surely die and become like water spilled on the ground, which cannot be gathered up again. Yet God does not take away life; but He devises means, so that His banished ones are not expelled from Him' (2 Sam. 14:14).

AVOID DISTRACTIONS

The evangelist must guard against distractions. It is abuse of the pulpit to preach politics, or even moral or social concerns; it is a failure of our stewardship of the gospel to make unnecessary hurdles to belief by preaching anything other than Christ and Him crucified. However, to speak of the character of God, or the sinfulness of humans, or the need to repent and believe, is not going to boost the preacher in the popularity charts. Even to speak of the uselessness of our own good works as far as salvation is concerned, rubs against the grain of people in our proud and self-sufficient age. Aware of this, it is easy for the evangelist to soften the blow of the gospel by over-emphasizing the joy, purpose and peace which is for those who will trust Christ. It *is* great to be a Christian. Christ *did* come that we might have life and have it more abundantly; but this is not the focus of our message.

Similarly, I feel concerned when I hear evangelists telling stories which are smutty, containing phrases which have *double entendres*, or are suggestive. Seeking to relate to our audience cannot justify behaving or speaking in an ungodly way. It is a contradiction to the gospel which we are seeking to proclaim (Eph. 5:12; Phil. 4:8).

The Welsh revival of 1904-1905 did not last for long, though its impact was great. Many of the men converted through the revival were distracted into socialism, and then, less than a decade later, the First World War wrought havoc in families and churches as so many young Christian men were called up and killed in the line of duty. According to *The Journal of Presbyterian History* (volume 51 (2), 1973), when Billy Sunday, the famous American evangelist, reached New York in 1917, his war against sin took a less important place as he threw his energy behind the American war effort. Unqualified patriotism became the virtue of virtues to him. His sermons, prayers and actions reflected the amalgamation of American religion and patriotism. Examples such as these serve as a timely reminder to keep to the basics. For the evangelist, the main thing is that the main thing is to be the main thing!

David Larsen says:

> The double foci of the Spirit's witness to the unconverted seem to be conviction for sin (John 16:8-11) and God's remedy for our sin and guilt in the finished work of Jesus Christ on the cross (John 12:32-33 and Rom. 3:21-26). In our day of no-fault accidents and no-fault divorce and instant solutions and 'I'm OK, you're OK' philosophy, there is considerable resistance to preaching against sin and preaching on the cross of Christ where God's wrath against sin was climatically disclosed and where His saving solution for sin was provided.

But this is the message which we need to preach from the pulpits and cry from the housetops. 1 Thessalonians 1:9-10 says: 'For they themselves declare concerning us what manner of entry we had to you, and how you turned to God from idols to serve the living and true God, and to wait for His Son from heaven, whom He raised from the dead, even Jesus who delivers us from the wrath to come.'

According to Romans 14:9, Christ did not die and rise to forgive us, or to buy a place in heaven for us, or that we might have peace and joy, but that 'He might be Lord of both the dead and the living'. Our tendency is to see the cross from the point of view of all the benefits we receive from Christ's suffering. In fact, Christ died to provide us with the only way we can be right with and related to God. Love, joy, peace, guidance and purpose are spin-offs of that spiritual life we have in Christ. There are believers who are persecuted and martyred for the cause of Christ. Their earthly, material, tangible gains are minimal, but they have eternal riches in Christ, which are more valuable than the entire world.

PAVING THE WAY TO THE CROSS

The evangelist is to speak of Christ, and call people to repentance and faith. Evangelism is, as someone said, 'the outreaching hand and heart of the people of God'. Paul wrote, 'I determined not to know anything among you except Jesus Christ and Him crucified' (1 Cor. 2:2). There is something about the person of Jesus Christ which is faith-creating. 'Preach Christ – He is preachable,' said Ed Hill in his inimitable way at the Amsterdam conference for itinerant evangelists in 1983. John Wesley, as an older man, spent less time denouncing sin and more time announcing Christ.

For the gospel to have been preached faithfully, the hidden work of Christ on the cross needs to be explained: that Christ carried the weight of the world's sin on His own shoulders. He died paying the penalty it would take us all eternity to pay. '[The] Father has sent the Son as Saviour of the world' (1 John 4:14). God looked back to the beginning of time in the Garden of Eden, and forward in time to the end, whenever that will be, and took the sin of the world, laying it on Christ on the cross. (See Isa. 53:6; Rom. 5:8; 1 Pet. 2:24; 3:18). 'God was in Christ, reconciling the world to Himself' (2 Cor. 5:19). This is the message we must get across to the world. But it may not be the message that the world wants.

In 1999, when the Church of England commissioned pollsters to find what the population of the UK would like from church, one correspondent wrote to *The Daily Telegraph* and said: 'We cannot be sure of what the replies will be, but we can be certain that repentance will not be one of the "wants". When will the contemporary churches learn that it is not what the people want that matters, but what Almighty God requires?'

Every evangelistic message should pave the way to the cross, for the cross is central to the revelation of God. Gardener Spring in his book *The Glory of the Cross* said:

> When Jesus stood a prisoner at the bar of Rome, He made the following, impressive, exalting avowal, 'To this end was I born and for this cause came I into the world that I might bear witness to the truth.' The cross was designed to be the most compendious and vivid expression of all religious truth. It is the great witness for the truth of God...every truth in the Bible brings us at last to the cross. The cross carries us back to every truth in the Bible. The sum and substance of every truth in the Bible is most impressively proved, illustrated and enforced by Christ and Him crucified. A right conception of what is included in the cross ensures a right conception of every important doctrine contained in the Bible. This is the hinge on which the whole system turns and the great truth alone by which any and all truths are understood.

Repentance and faith are inseparably linked together. John the Baptist and the Lord Jesus preached repentance (Mark 1:4; 6:12;

Luke 13:3). It was repentance and faith that Christ said would be preached to all nations (Luke 24:46-47). These twin truths are a major theme in the book of Acts (2:38; 3:19; 5:31; 8:22; 11:18), in the preaching of Paul (Acts 17:30; 20:21; 26:19, 20) and the epistles (for example, Heb. 6:1; 2 Pet: 3:9). Paul used the word 'gospel' at least 70 times. He was committed to the preaching of the gospel, and driven by the good news of Christ.

The nature of preaching the cross will include the following facts. Humans are separated from God by sin (Isa. 59:2). Jesus, the Son of God, was sent by God to provide the remedy. This was accomplished by His sin-bearing (1 Pet. 2:24). He was made a curse for us (Gal. 3:13, quoting Deut. 21:23). Apostolic preaching referred to 'the tree' in this sense (Acts 5:30; 10:39). Peter was obviously fond of the expression: 'who Himself bore our sins in His own body on the tree, that we, having died to sins, might live for righteousness – by whose stripes you are healed' (1 Pet. 2:24). Jesus was raised from the dead on the third day (1 Cor. 15:1-4). Whenever Jesus spoke about His crucifixion, He also spoke about His resurrection (for example, Mark 8:31; 10:33-34). The consequences of this are that we have forgiveness through Christ (Acts 10:43); we are justified (Acts 13:34-39; Rom. 5:1) and we have a new life and inheritance by the Holy Spirit (Acts 26:18; 5:32). On the basis of this, we need to persuade men and women to repent and believe (Acts 26:20; 2:38-39; 1 Thess. 1:9-10). The 'evangel' has to be in evangelism! Our task is to tell people about God, good news and grace.

'Know your subject, be yourself and love your audience' are the three rules for good communication according to Josh McDowell. In our own individual style, we are to convey the truths of the gospel to others. The truth we communicate will outlast us. As communicators of truth we have no right to twist it to woo an audience. 'Let God be true, but every man a liar'

(Rom. 3:4). As our minds are to be full of the truth of the gospel, our hearts should be on fire with the sheer glory of the message. It will grieve us deeply when people turn away from it but there will be an overwhelming joy when people turn from their sin to trust Christ. The thrill of seeing people converted is almost beyond compare. Keep close to the Lord and that joy will not lessen with time.

A SIMPLE GOSPEL

Martin Luther said, 'The common people are captivated more readily by comparisons and examples than by difficult and subtle disputations. They would rather see a well-drawn picture than a well-written book.' Warren Wiersbe expresses the same insight differently, 'People's minds are picture galleries, not debating chambers.' In his book *Preaching and Teaching with Imagination* Wiersbe argues that in communicating the Word of God we should turn people's ears into eyes, so they can 'see the truth'. The evangelist will want to express the truths of the gospel as simply as possible.

Simplicity does not mean, however, that we insult the intelligence of the more academic or philosophical. T. C. Hammond, the great Irish theologian, said: 'I believe in a simple gospel, but not a silly gospel.' We need the likes of Francis Schaeffer and Ravi Zacharias in our world where so many voices are seeking to capture the mindset of society. Schaeffer exposed and answered the philosophies which are the foundation of our current society. R. A.Torrey was a logician, Josh McDowell is an apologist, but both powerfully convey the gospel very clearly and simply. I remember hearing the late Prof. Sir J. N. D. Anderson (Professor of Oriental Laws and Director of the Institute of Advanced Legal Studies in the University of London). His vocabulary was virtually monosyllabic, and his presentation of the gospel could not have been clearer or more thorough. There was power in his simplicity.

Paul wrote:

> For Christ did not send me to baptize, but to preach the gospel, not with wisdom of words, lest the cross of Christ should be made of no effect. For the message of the cross is foolishness to those who are perishing, but to us who are being saved, it is the power of God. For it is written:
>
>> 'I will destroy the wisdom of the wise,
>> And bring to nothing the understanding of the prudent.'
>
> Where is the wise? Where is the scribe? Where is the disputer of this age? Has not God made foolish the wisdom of this world? For since, in the wisdom of God, the world through wisdom did not know God, it pleased God through the foolishness of the message preached to save those who believe. For Jews request a sign, and Greeks seek after wisdom; but we preach Christ crucified, to the Jews a stumbling block and to the Greeks foolishness, but to those who are called, both Jews and Greeks, Christ the power of God and the wisdom of God. Because the foolishness of God is wiser than men, and the weakness of God is stronger than men.... But God has chosen the foolish things of the world to put to shame the wise, and God has chosen the weak things of the world to put to shame the things which are mighty; and the base things of the world and the things which are despised God has chosen, and the things which are not, to bring to nothing the things that are, that no flesh should glory in His presence...that, as it is written, 'He who glories, let him glory in the Lord.' And I, brethren, when I came to you, did not come with excellence of speech or of wisdom declaring to you the testimony of God. For I determined not to know anything among you except Jesus Christ and Him crucified'. (1 Cor. 1:17–2:2)

AN EARNEST HEART

As much as possible, seek to jettison the jargon and assume that people have no religious background or understanding. Present the gospel using a Bible story, doctrine, passage or verse. Pray that it will remain in the minds of the hearers, and you will find that it will also feed and bless the hearts of the Christian people listening. The aim, though, is not to tickle the ears of believers with fascinating new biblical insights, but to so proclaim the gospel that the unbeliever will understand the message. Then God, the Holy Spirit, can take hold of the truths and forcibly apply them, with conviction, to the unconverted. Paul Bassett says, 'A convicting gospel must be preached. The evangelist is not a comedian, or entertainer, but one who convicts.' Earnestness in preaching is not put on as an act, but is an expression of deep concern for lost men and women. Robert Murray McCheyne spent his Saturdays visiting the sick and dying in Dundee where he ministered, not only to be a blessing to them, but to prepare his own heart for ministry in his church the next day. The preparation of the heart is as vital as the preaching to the hearts of men and women.

The Word of God and the Spirit of God working together brings life out of death. As we preach the Word, God works in the hearts of the hearer to bring about re-birth. If a Christian is critical because he feels that the evangelist is going along well-trodden paths, it is only because there is a misunderstanding of the work of the evangelist whose duty and joy it is to speak of foundational truths (cf. Heb. 5:12). The evangelist will lovingly warn people of the judgment they deserve and the way of escape found in Christ.

For such a work, there will inevitably need to be a strong devotional life. Someone has said, 'You're never preaching until the audience hears another voice.' The work of the evangelist involves and includes time spent alone with God in a consistent and disciplined way. 'Power from a fresh, daily anointing of the Holy Spirit in the time you are alone with God is the product of a healthy devotional life. There is no shortcut to such power in the ministry. Nor do we ever reach a point in our ministries where this is no longer needed,' said Billy Graham. It was said of Finney that 'he prepared his sermons, but most of all he prepared himself.' Job said that he desired the words of the Lord's mouth more than his necessary food (Job 23:12). The daily 'quiet time' should be an indispensable part of the day, a vital prerequisite before any ministry. This is no more legalistic than ensuring that our bodies are receiving sufficient food for all that we demand of them. As evangelists, we are to be people of the Book. We should love it, read it, know it, discuss it, preach it and live it. It should flow through our thinking and reasoning so that out of the abundance of our hearts our mouths will speak. The Word and prayer are married together, and what God has joined together we should not put asunder. Out of that marriage will come the fruit of biblical, powerful, gospel preaching, which the Lord can use and bless.

15 Some contentious issues

Phillips Brooks defined preaching as 'truth through personality'. The Lord uses individuals with their individuality, so it is inevitable that there will be a variety of means of spreading the gospel. Snide criticism and cynicism of others' methods have done damage to the spirit of genuine love and unity which we ought to be enjoying as fellow believers. Remember, despite the fact that the gospel was preached from wrong motives, the apostle Paul delighted in the fact that at least the Word was getting out: 'Some indeed preach Christ even from envy and strife, and some also from goodwill: the former preach Christ from selfish ambition, not sincerely, supposing to add affliction to my chains; but the latter out of love, knowing that I am appointed for the defence of the gospel. What then? Only that in every way, whether in pretense or in truth, Christ is preached; and in this I rejoice, yes, and will rejoice' (Phil. 1:15-18). Such magnanimity is rarely seen in Christian workers, where professional jealousy can be a destructive power for evil. Controversy and criticism should be used to fine-tune the evangelist, not to finish off his ministry. However, as much as is in us, we should strive to be biblical in our methods as well as our message and motives.

UNITY IN PRIMARY ISSUES

Those who are evangelistic must be evangelical. Those we work with in evangelism must believe the gospel. There needs to be doctrinal purity in our fellowship and in the counselling room. There does not necessarily have to be agreement on all our particulars of Christian belief, but surely we have to be united in the basic issues such as the final authority of the Bible, the nature of the Triune God, the Deity of the Lord Jesus, the finished work of Christ on the cross, His bodily resurrection and eventual return to this earth, and the reality of heaven and hell. Let us not forget the warning from Paul: 'But even if we, or an angel from heaven, should preach any gospel to you other than what we have preached to you, let him be accursed. As we have said before, so now I say again, if anyone preaches any gospel to you other than what you have received, let him be accursed' (Gal. 1:8-9). This truth needs to be kept in balance with the words of Christ in John 13:34-35: 'A new commandment I give to you, that you love one another; as I have loved you, that you also love one another. By this all will know that you are My disciples, if you have love for one another.' We dare not sacrifice truth on the altar of love, nor love on the altar of truth. Neither should evangelism be sacrificed for petty foibles and squabbles. Current expediency could well be creating a long-term fall out, the devastating effects of which may not be felt until another generation; but to neglect to evangelize is to turn our backs on the pressing needs of people who need the Lord, and whose children and grandchildren need the Lord.

Thus, unity in the primary issues is essential. There are, however, a number of what could be called 'secondary' areas in the work of evangelism which have caused contention. These are (1) the invitation, (2) itinerancy and (3) music. I would like to spend the rest of this chapter looking at these contentious issues.

THE INVITATION

Is it the evangelist's responsibility to urge and lead people to respond there and then to the gospel? Is it right to put loving pressure (not coercion) on people to bring them to the Lord? If it is right to plead with people during a message, why not at the end of the sermon? Evangelists have been criticized for being too emotional, or too prolonged in their appealing. Emotion is not wrong in itself as long as it is generated by God and His Word. Some evangelists have been guilty of deceit, others of trying to make up in their appeal for what they haven't done in their message. Having preached powerlessly, they make a long drawn-out appeal. We deplore these abuses and fear that instead of 'bringing people to birth' they are producing spiritual miscarriages. It cannot be right to give what may be false assurance to those who publicly respond in any way, by telling them that they are now saved. I have heard this described as 'Protestant absolution!' However, abuses should not prevent us from correctly using means which can be blessed of God.

PARABLES FROM WHICH TO LEARN

It is worth going over Jesus' parable of the great supper for it provides us with a good model:

> A certain man gave a great supper and invited many, and sent his
> servant at supper time to say to those who were invited, 'Come,

for all things are now ready.' But they all with one accord began to make excuses. The first said to him, 'I have bought a piece of ground, and I must go and see it. I ask you to have me excused.' And another said, 'I have bought five yoke of oxen, and I am going to test them. I ask you to have me excused.' Still another said, 'I have married a wife, and therefore I cannot come.' So that servant came and reported these things to his master. Then the master of the house, being angry, said to his servant, 'Go out quickly into the streets and lanes of the city, and bring in here the poor and the maimed and the lame and the blind.' And the servant said, 'Master, it is done as you commanded, and still there is room.' Then the master said to the servant, 'Go out into the highways and hedges, and compel them to come in, that my house may be filled.' (Luke 14:16-23)

In the parable, there are three types of people: those you would expect to come at the invitation, those who have to be persuaded, and those who have to be compelled to come. It is worth noting that the Good News did not fit into the lives of people in the times of Christ either! Samuel R. Schutz of Gordon-Conwell Seminary says there are four groups of people to whom we minister the gospel: (1) sceptics, who are the unreceptive; (2) prodigals, who are converted but backslidden; (3) seekers, who are receptive but, as yet, unconverted; and (4) pilgrims, who are believers making progress in the Lord. An appeal needs to be appropriate to each type of person. Some are more sensitive or inhibited than others, and we should ensure that they are not put off by brashness, but we need not fear being earnest. One unconverted man said of D. L. Moody, 'He talked to me about my soul as though it mattered!'

In trying to find the balance, various evangelists have brought their messages to a conclusion in differing ways, but the point is, *we should preach and work with the expectation of seeing people converted*. We must constantly remind ourselves that 'salvation is of the LORD' (Jonah 2:9). As somebody expressed it: God thought it, God bought it, God brought it, God taught it and I caught it! Ultimately, therefore, the evangelist cannot save a single soul. That is God's work, but He uses people, strategies, methods and messages. Campbell Morgan said, 'We are out to storm the citadel of the will and seize it for Jesus Christ.' James Stewart, quoting Henry Ward Beecher, argued: 'A sermon is not a Chinese fire-cracker to be fired off for the noise it makes. It is the hunter's gun, and at every discharge, he should look to see his game fall.'

We know from the parable of the sower (Matt. 13:3-9, 18-23), as well as from painful experience, that not all the people we speak to about Christ will be converted. 2 Corinthians 2:15 and 16 explains what happens: 'For we are to God the fragrance of Christ among those who are being saved and among those who are perishing. To the one we are the aroma of death to death, and to the other the aroma of life to life. And who is sufficient for these things?' David Larsen in his book, *The Evangelism Mandate*, calls the appeal the 'R.S.V.P.' of the gospel, and quotes this verse:

> One ship drives east, another west,
> With the self-same winds that blow.
> 'Tis the set of the sail, and not the gale
> That tells them the way to go.

VARIOUS METHODS

Our desire, though, is that all should come to know the true and living God as they turn from their idols. We will find ourselves pleading with and urging everyone to trust Christ as Lord and Saviour. After all, if we do not lovingly constrain people to trust Christ, who will? The film maker Ken Anderson has on his business card the motto: 'If not me, who? – if not now, when?'

Personality, setting, theological conviction, and the era and culture in which we live, will determine which method of appeal is most appropriate, but appeal we must.

Anthony of Padua would invite people to throw vestiges of the old life into a bonfire. Bernard of Clairvaux would ask people to raise their hands to indicate their conversion to Christ. Jonathan Edwards advocated earnest pleading with sinners. C. H. Spurgeon used the inquiry room and personally interviewed converts before baptizing them or admitting them as church members. He enthusiastically backed the D. L. Moody evangelistic meetings. Spurgeon's successor at the Metropolitan Tabernacle, Dr A. C. Dixon, asked seekers 'to come forward'. Charles G. Finney used the mourner's bench and the inquirer's room. Billy Graham basically gives the invitation in the opening prayer, and throughout his message is urging a response until he finally asks people 'to get up out of their seats and come forward'. Dr Martyn Lloyd Jones, when ministering in Sandfields, would meet after the evening service with people who would come to sit in the front pews, and later at Westminster Chapel he would receive people one by one in his office, just as a doctor would in his surgery.

My usual method, which is designed to be suitable for the typically reserved English audiences, is to ask people to come immediately after the meeting and ask me or, for example, the pastor of the church, for a pack which contains counselling materials; and I introduce them to a Christian of the same sex who will speak with them. David Larsen says, 'Scripture, church history, theology, and psychology, as well as practical issues facing the church today, uphold the legitimacy of a public response to Christ in many settings and situations despite the dangers and pitfalls that surround us. Isn't this the story of Christian ministry at all times and in every place?'

There is a very real fear for many evangelists that there will be little or no response when an appeal is made to trust Christ, and that is embarrassing. It is possible to find oneself in the position that Isaiah experienced, that the children are brought to birth, but we do not have the strength to deliver them (Isa. 37:3). However, to offer a counselling pack with evangelistic and follow-up literature with a Gospel or New Testament can be a way of overcoming the very open, public appeal or public pledge, as R. T. Kendall prefers to call the response. As you press the claims of Christ, you are doing so against the background of the work that Satan has been doing for years. Surely, the cross of Christ gives us the right to demand a response; after all, people cannot become more lost than they were previously.

BIBLICAL BASIS

Didn't God appeal directly to Adam in the Garden of Eden (Gen. 3:9)? Didn't Moses appeal to the rebellious and disobedient Israelites asking, 'Whoever is on the LORD's side, let him come to me.' And didn't all the Levites respond (Exod. 32:26)? Didn't Joshua appeal to the Israelites asking for public response: 'And if it seems evil to you to serve the LORD, choose for yourselves this day whom you will serve, whether the gods which your fathers served...or the gods of the Amorites, in whose land you dwell. But as for me and my house, we will serve the LORD.' So the people answered and said: 'Far be it from us that we should forsake the LORD to serve other gods...' (Josh. 24:15-16). Didn't Elijah appeal to the people on Mount Carmel (1 Kings 18:21), and Josiah call for a response (2 Kings 23:3)?

The same earnest appealing was found in Ezra, Nehemiah, Joel, Jonah and many of the prophets, who were expressing the loving appeal of a tender and compassionate God (for example, Isaiah 1:18: '"Come now, and let us reason together," says the Lord, "Though your sins are like scarlet, they shall be as white as snow; though they are red like crimson, they shall be as wool,"' and Ezekiel 33:11: 'Say to them: "As I live," says the LORD GOD, "I have no pleasure in the death of the wicked, but that the wicked turn from his way and live. Turn, turn from your evil ways! For why should you die, O house of Israel?"')

The Lord Jesus invited men and women to leave their sins and follow Him publicly. As Billy Graham has so often said, every person that Jesus asked to follow Him, was asked publicly. Think, for example, of Zacchaeus to whom Christ said, in effect, 'Come down, come home, come now, come as you are!' (Luke 19:5, 6). When Jesus healed the woman with the flow of blood, He asked, 'Who touched Me?' No doubt the question was to give her the assurance that she had not 'stolen' blessing from Jesus, but He did ask for public confession (Luke 8:43-48). The same pattern is found throughout the New Testament. We read of three thousand, and then five thousand people accepting the message and the Lord Jesus Christ on the day of Pentecost and later. Peter said, 'Be saved from this perverse generation' (Acts 2:40) and many believed (Acts 2:41; 4:4). This definite response continues throughout the book of Acts – see 5:14; 6:1, 7; 8:6, 12; 10:44, 48; 11:21, 24; 12:24. A physical, outward response often confirms what has happened inwardly. It shows the Lord, others and the responder the definiteness of the response to the claims of Christ on their lives.

Pleading with men and women to repent and believe the gospel is serious work. I never like to hear jokes about these moments in a message. We are on sacred territory. There will be an inward agony of soul and deep desire for the lost. This part of the ministry is quite exhausting. It is acting as a spiritual midwife, and one needs patience, tenderness and a yearning for the souls of men and women. We need God in all our work, but particularly as we invite and urge people to trust Christ.

Itinerancy

Should the evangelist be locally based, or is there a place for the itinerant evangelist?

Philip is the only named evangelist of the Bible, and we can see from his example that there is a place for both. We read of Philip initially working as an itinerant evangelist, preaching to great effect in Samaria, then being led by the Spirit of God into the wilderness to lead the Ethiopian eunuch to Christ, then in Azotus and preaching 'in all the cities till he came to Caesarea' (Acts 8:4-40). Later, we find that he settled in Caesarea itself (Acts 21:8) and ministered there for about twenty years. Significantly, we read that he had four daughters; maybe they were the reason why he settled down.

Certainly it is not easy to cope with the pressure of leaving one's family constantly; however, the Lord has made special promises for those who do make such a sacrifice: 'And everyone who has left houses or brothers or sisters or father or mother or wife or children or lands, for My name's sake, shall receive a hundredfold, and inherit everlasting life' (Matt. 19:29). Speaking personally, I have found long absences away from home the hardest part of my ministry, and I have never got used to this aspect of itinerant evangelism. I fear I am not being a good husband to my wife, or father to my four children. Although people are usually very hospitable, living out of a suitcase in other people's homes is never quite the same as being at home. I remind myself of promises such as Jesus' word that 'whoever loses his life for My sake will save it' (Luke 9:24). I have a rule of thumb, which I try to stick to, not to be away from home for more than three weeks at one time, though this does not always work out. David Wyrtzen in his book *Unexpected Grace*, honestly and touchingly recalls what it meant to him to be brought up as the son of a well-known evangelist. Nobody would want to criticize Jack Wyrtzen, for the Lord has greatly used him, but there are timely reminders here:

> I wasn't raised in the home of an Old Testament patriarch, but my father's renown as an evangelist made me think so at times. Dad poured his whole life into building a worldwide evangelistic organisation. He lived to preach the gospel, and there was little relationship energy left for Mom's emotional needs, or for us five children.
>
> By my freshman year in college my mother was tired – emotionally, physically and spiritually. A frail body and the years of carrying most of the daily burden in raising a family alone had become too much. I remember sitting in her bedroom and listening as she cried, 'Dave, your father is married to his work. I'm tired of competing with Word of Life. I'm going to get in the car and leave. Maybe I'll get a divorce. We'll see how successful he is as an evangelist with divorce papers sitting on his desk.'
>
> ...It was difficult to realise that Dad and Mom were only normal, middle-aged people facing the problems that many workaholic executives create.... But the real Jesus never failed, and His grace rescued me and my family.

Samuel, as a judge in Israel, followed an itinerant pattern on a regular route: 'So Samuel judged Israel all the days of his life. He went from year to year on a circuit to Bethel, Gilgal, and Mizpah, and judged Israel in all those places. But he always returned to Ramah, for his home was there. There he judged Israel, and there he built an altar to the Lord' (1 Sam. 7:15-17). Some have suggested that his itinerant work was the reason that his children did not follow in their father's faith and walk with God. This is not clear from the passage, though there are obvious dangers for the family life of itinerant workers. However, if God calls, he equips and honours those who honour Him. There are many examples of the children of itinerant evangelists growing up to be a credit to their parents and their parents' God. In my repeated and prolonged absences from home whilst involved in evangelism in my own country or overseas, I have claimed for my children the promise of Psalm 68:5, that God would be a 'Father of the fatherless, a defender of widows'. The itinerant, preaching evangelist needs an understanding and committed spouse who is not going to undermine or criticize her partner in the many absences, but instead will feed positive attitudes both to him and their children. God is to be Lord of the evangelist's calling and the evangelist's partner's calling. God will amply reward both (see 1 Sam. 30:24).

Itinerants are sometimes criticized for not understanding the pressures and the mundaneness of a settled ministry, or of regular church life. To some extent this is inevitable. But even the itinerant will have his own particular friends who will be cared for by the evangelist. The evangelist will also spend a fair amount of time with pastors, listening to and learning from them. Itinerant work is not escapist.

Of course, the ministry of Christ was an itinerant one, and He taught His disciples to itinerate (Luke 10:2ff.) because 'The harvest truly is great, but the labourers are few; therefore pray the Lord of the harvest to send out labourers into His harvest' (Luke 10:2). The apostle Paul was an itinerant preacher as he travelled on his three missionary journeys, although he did remain in the places where he was working for up to two years, until a church had been established there. In 2 Corinthians 8:18 we read of a well-respected travelling Christian who in all likelihood was an itinerant evangelist.

There are many problems and expenses which can be avoided if an evangelist can be locally based. He can be involved in evangelizing and spearheading evangelistic work in a locality. The message of the evangelist is ideally suited for itinerating, and perhaps an ideal is for a church or group of churches in a locality to employ an evangelist for their area, giving them the freedom to be involved in evangelistic missions further afield, at their own discretion or under the advice of their accountability-board. Surely churches which appoint pastors and youth leaders should seriously consider appointing evangelists, who will work alongside the leadership of the church but have particular responsibility for leading evangelistic endeavour, and training the church to be evangelistic. It appears a slightly selfish thing that we call people to look after our spiritual needs, but not those of the lost. We sneer at the words spoken to William Carey at his induction in Leicester in 1793, 'But if God purposes to save the heathen, will He not take steps to effect it Himself?'; but are we not guilty of acting like that in many of our churches? There is space for rich diversity in the Lord's work.

MUSIC

Significantly, many of the leading mass-evangelists in recent years have been closely attached to a song-leader or singer. Music has often been associated with revivals, such as the revival in Great Britain in the eighteenth century which gave birth to the hymns of Charles Wesley. Music is a powerful means of touching the emotions and stirring the spirit. It features both in Old and New Testament worship.

The reason why Christians sing is simple – they have something to sing about! There are songs in the Holy Bible, in the heart of the believer, and in heaven. Two themes swell the praises of heaven. There is praise for creation:

> You are worthy, O Lord,
> To receive glory and honour and power;
> For You created all things,
> And by Your will they exist and were created. (Rev. 4:11)

There is, however, another new song in heaven; that is praise for salvation:

> You are worthy...
> For You were slain
> And have redeemed us to God by Your blood,
> Out of every tribe and tongue and people and nation. (Rev. 5:9)

Godly music ministers to the preacher. In 2 Kings 3, it appears that it was only after music was played that Elisha could prophesy. I imagine that George Beverly Shea was ministering to Billy Graham as well as the vast crowds, as he sang immediately prior to Billy Graham preaching. But in our current secular age, is it now right, realistic or relevant to ask unsaved people to sing?

Good music is in itself a draw to unconverted people. If the music honours the Lord, it can, therefore, be a strong evangelistic tool. Music can be used by the Lord to speak to the unsaved. In a day and age when so much music has become worldly and dominated by the rhythm, which affects people physically more than spiritually, Christian music can and should be a testimony in itself. It can show the contrast between music which edifies and music which entertains. It introduces the unsaved into Christian worship and should encourage them to consider using their hearts and mouths to praise the Lord who at very least is their Creator, and we trust will become their personal Saviour. However, it is never to be a substitute for the preaching of the gospel. Evangelist and founder of Word of Life, Jack Wyrtzen, taught his musical son, Don, always to preach the gospel in every concert. It was good advice and he has kept to it.

16 The temptations of the evangelist

Anyone on the front line in a battle should expect to be fired at by the enemy. But sometimes 'friendly fire' can cause damage. The psychological and emotional condition of the soldiers, if not well cared for, can in itself be destructive, as was illustrated in the trenches of the First World War. The enemy within has to be guarded against, because Satan will use any and every ploy to undermine and even destroy the work of the evangelist. We must not be ignorant of his devices. Being forewarned should lead us to being forearmed. This is crucial for the evangelist. C. S. Lewis, in *The Screwtape Letters*, said, 'No one knows how bad he is until he has tried to be good. There is a silly idea about that good people don't know what temptation means.'

The standard outline summarizing the temptations of the evangelist has three points: pride, sex and money. Or for those who prefer alliteration: self, sex and silver; or: fame, females and fortune! As the body of Christ, we have had to hang our heads in shame too many times to be able to dismiss these three deadly weapons lightly, for Satan has used them repeatedly to such effect. However, I do not believe they are the whole story. To limit Satan, the supreme cynic, is to blinker oneself to his subtleties and absolute commitment to seek to destroy every work of God. We need to examine some of his many devices, and that is what I hope to do in the course of this chapter.

Money can be irresistible, and that is why Christ warned about the desire for things (Mark 4:19); Paul wrote of the evils of the love of money (1 Tim. 6:10), and how he resisted the danger of becoming a peddler of the Word of God: 'For we are not, like so many, peddling the word of God; but as of sincerity, but as from God, we speak in the sight of God in Christ' (2 Cor. 2:17). With passing phases and trends certain words and concepts become unfashionable in Christian circles. One of these in today's society is the word 'sacrifice'. Jesus said, 'If anyone desires to come after Me, let him deny himself, and take up his cross daily, and follow Me' (Luke 9:23). Paul wrote, 'But godliness with contentment is great gain. For we brought nothing into this world, and it is certain we can carry nothing out. And having food and clothing, with these we shall be content. But those who desire to be rich fall into temptation and a snare, and into many foolish and harmful lusts which drown men in destruction and perdition' (1 Tim. 6:6-9).

The temptation to prosper from the gospel shows itself in many ways – a desire to stay in the best houses when away from home, or even the insistence upon staying in smart hotels; wanting to work with richer churches or cultivating wealthy contacts; a craving for more things and possessions, each legitimate in itself, but each adding to the weight we are carrying around; a forgetfulness that as riches increase, so does the responsibility to give more.

There needs to be financial accountability, so that evangelists do not fall prey to the temptation to manipulate the figures for the tax man, or pocket that which was given for the ministry and should be accounted for – 'not pilfering, but showing all good fidelity' (Titus 2:10). How can we expect God to bless when such practices are going on? Are we really willing to sell our ministry for a few pounds or dollars?

For some, the struggle can be to make ends meet. I know full-time evangelists who live on next to nothing. For these people the temptation to become bitter towards those who have more, or who could give more, is very real. Hudson Taylor said, 'God's work, done in God's way will not lack God's supply', and it is true that God will supply all our needs according to His riches in Christ Jesus, but it is also true that certain people and ministries attract more money than others. Those whose charismatic personality can appeal for cash will usually find some Christian who will support them. We praise God for such support, but those who do not ask can be discouraged and even envy those who do. Our hearts are deceitful, and we need to remind ourselves why we are evangelizing: 'For the grace of God that brings salvation has appeared to all men, teaching us that, denying ungodliness and worldly lusts, we should live soberly, righteously, and godly in the present age, looking for the blessed hope and glorious appearing of our great God and Saviour Jesus Christ, who gave Himself for us, that He might redeem us from every lawless deed and purify for Himself His own special people, zealous for good works' (Titus 2:11-14).

Whichever way Satan tempts us in the area of finance, it is important to remember they are distortions of reality; he is twisting the truth to wreck a ministry. Agur's wise prayer is a word which bears repetition, 'Give me neither poverty nor riches – Feed me with the food You prescribe for me' (Prov. 30:8).

It is neither wise nor spiritual to claim that our materialistic era permits us to live differently from the example and commands of Christ, or the sacrificial dedication of His followers. Jesus who was rich, for our sakes became poor. He was born in a manger, preached from a borrowed boat, had to ask for a coin to illustrate a truth, rode to Jerusalem on a borrowed donkey, and was buried in another's tomb. He said, 'Foxes have holes and birds of the air have nests, but the Son of Man has nowhere to lay His head' (Luke 9:58). His only possession, His garment, was gambled for at the time of His crucifixion. He frequently denounced riches and warned of covetousness. The disciple has no right to be above his Master (Matt 10:24-25).

Once I had the privilege of preaching to a group of young men and women in their twenties working with Operation Mobilisation in Secondrabad, in India. They were about to go to work in one of India's shanty towns, where there is no running water, sanitation or electricity and the people live in huts, covered with corrugated iron. These evangelists would be living with the shanty town dwellers because they knew they could not evangelize effectively from a distance. Such people are a challenge to us and the Christian church.

C. T. Studd, cricketer and missionary pioneer, wrote: 'I had known about Jesus dying for me, but I had never understood that if He died for me, then I didn't belong to myself. Redemption means buying back, so that if I belonged to Him, either I had to be a thief and keep what wasn't mine, or else I had to give up everything to God. When I came to see that Jesus Christ had died for me, it didn't seem hard to give up all for Him.'

To keep money in perspective means being accountable to others and God, remembering that, whereas we want to accumulate things, Christ emptied Himself on our behalf. Let us seek to be people known for our integrity (2 Cor. 3:1-3).

SEX

'Open sin has killed its thousands, but secret sin its ten thousands,' said Bishop J. C. Ryle of Liverpool. The trouble is that secret sin eventually leads to open sin. There are too many former Christian leaders who have moved away from areas of Christian service because they chose the pleasures of sin for a season. They fell prey to a temptation Scripture repeatedly warns about. The possibility of this sin is so real that we need the Lord's daily grace and strength to resist temptations and keep ourselves pure: 'Be sober, be vigilant, because your adversary the devil walks about like a roaring lion, seeking whom he may devour. Resist him, steadfast in the faith...' (1 Pet. 5:8-9). The Lord's desire is not primarily for gifted evangelists, but for *godly* evangelists.

Because of the personality and nature of the work of the evangelist, he is likely to have a strong sex drive. Passion manifests itself in many ways – spiritual and sensual. The evangelist should know what to run from and what to guard against when it comes to sexual matters. Joseph (in Genesis 39) is a model of fleeing when temptation came, even though it cost him thirteen years of incarceration in an Egyptian cell. In contrast Samson played with fire...and got burnt. Better to run than be ruined. There is the straightforward choice, made daily in the strength of the Lord, to refuse to watch 'adult' videos or certain television programmes, not to look at suggestive pictures in newspapers or magazines, to keep a distance from people of the opposite sex and similar age, and certainly not to be alone with them, even in a counselling situation. Flee from such settings.

Evangelists need to guard themselves from fantasizing and daydreaming when the mind is idle. Lust, in the Lord's sight, is adultery. We need to guard ourselves from the flattery of foolish people who are drawn to us simply because we are in the forefront of Christian service. Henry Martyn, a missionary, used to transform his admiration for any beautiful woman into a prayer, silently asking the Lord to make her as beautiful on the inside as she was on the outside. I have found that idea helpful. Feed the mind with the things of God and seek to make progress for Him (Phil. 4:8).

There really is no substitute for the daily, dogged, delightful discipline of having time with God. Those cumulated hours of meditation, study and prayer keep the heart in tune to live melodiously for Him. Study Proverbs 5, Malachi 2:13-16 and 1 Thessalonians 4:1-8, and prove that 'we are more than conquerors through Him' (Rom. 8:37), remembering always that 'the blood of Jesus Christ His Son cleanses us from all sin' (1 John 1:7). God has given lifelong spouses as companions so that our natural affections and passions may be channelled correctly. This is such a valuable way of escape that Satan will attack our homes. The balance between service and responsibilities at home is hard to maintain, but love is to be cultivated. Walter Trobisch said, 'Marriage is not an achievement which is finished. It is a dynamic process between two people, a relation which is constantly being changed, which grows or dies.' A good wife/husband will be a great protector against this area of temptation.

As Warren Wiersbe says: 'There are two ways to get money out of a bank. You can rob the bank, creating a whole new set of problems for yourself; or you can become a depositor, commit yourself to the bank, and have the privilege of making use of its assets. Sex outside marriage is like robbing the bank. Marriage is the commitment that enriches life as husband and wife live together in the will of God.'

PRIDE

Oswald Chambers said, 'It is easy to be shocked at immorality, but how much education in the school of Christ, how much reliance on the Holy Spirit, does it take to bring us to the place where we are shocked at pride against God? That sensitivity is lacking today.' Evangelists, as all other leaders, are to avoid pride, especially the pride of the person 'up front' (1 Tim. 3:6; 2 Tim. 2:24-25).

Let us remind ourselves, first of all, that our salvation is a gift from God and not earned by our own works, no matter how faithful or sacrificial (see Rom. 6:23; Eph. 2:8-9 and Titus 3:5-8). Any gifting which an evangelist has is a gift from God. 1 Corinthians 4:7 makes this point clear: 'For who makes you differ from another? And what do you have that you did not receive? Now if you did indeed receive it, why do you glory as if you had not received it?'

Pride encourages us to seek popularity, longing to be well thought of and spoken about. The snare of being men-pleasers rather than God-pleasers is always there. It can lead evangelists to 'play to the gallery', committing the blasphemy of manipulating the service and the work of God to further their own egos. Telling a series of humorous stories can communicate, but it can also enhance ego and lead to the preaching of a soft gospel. Paul warns Timothy against this in 2 Timothy 1:13-14, exhorting him to 'Hold fast the pattern of sound words which you have heard from me...' Pride encourages the evangelist to be 'with it' rather than to be faithful. Pride may even cause the preacher to flatter the congregation, drawing attention to self rather than Christ. Pride will lead the evangelist to be selective in the people he speaks with, counselling only those he is naturally attracted to or impressed by, but ignoring the poor and unlovely, forgetting that the common people heard Jesus gladly.

In the busy-ness of life, evangelists may find that they begin to lose individual concern for people, and can develop a self-centred attitude that may lead to a lack of consideration of the needs of the pastors and church leaders with whom they are working. If others do not quite share the same vision, we may become intolerant, or even jealous. At such times it is good to remember John 21, with its threefold emphasis: catch fish, feed sheep and mind your own business (see verse 23). Looking around can be discouraging, whereas looking up is most encouraging.

In the specialized use of gifts, perhaps others will help set out halls, clear up after events and be involved in mundane administrative work, but in the interests of crucifying self and seeking humility it is helpful for the evangelist to be involved in 'foot washing' in whatever way is appropriate in that particular situation. Christ is our example in this (Phil. 2:5-9). Again the value of a good spouse who will lovingly criticize is inestimable, as is a group of fellow Christians to whom one is accountable and in whom one has implicit trust. Their honesty should be encouraged as that will help to keep the evangelist humble.

The evangelist will receive plenty of criticism. Some of this is simply fighting talk from people who love to squabble, but much of what is being said or written against the evangelist may well be valid. After all, the evangelist is human, and therefore bound to make mistakes. Criticism, though it can hurt, can be turned into real blessing. Use it as an instrument from the Lord and others to break down pride. Read the letter, listen to the critics and hear their whispers. Instead of instantly reacting to defend oneself, allow twenty-four hours to ponder what has been said. Others' insights may be a real blessing and will help to keep you humble. Sometimes we may feel we have to defend ourselves, but more often than not we can listen in silence. Warren Wiersbe once thanked a person who had written to him and then added, 'Your letter must have been hard to write wearing boxing gloves!'

The Bible does not allow us to be proud. Evangelism and the winning of souls are the work of God. We read in 1 Corinthians 3:6-8: 'I planted, Apollos watered, but God gave the increase. So then neither he who plants is anything, nor he who waters, but God who gives the increase.' William Grimshaw, the eighteenth-century Anglican clergyman, who saw thousands converted in Yorkshire and beyond, said on his deathbed, 'Here goes an unprofitable servant.'

THE SUCCESS FACTOR

The need to be 'successful' may warp the perspective of the evangelist. Our calling is to preach the gospel to the lost, and we must not allow anything to distract us from that.

As an evangelist, I would always seek to present the gospel in a sensible way at every opportunity – at weddings, funerals, best-man's speeches, school speech days, anniversaries, carol services and the like. It is all too easy to become a 'preacher' rather than an evangelist, especially if one has built up a reputation and is in demand to 'fill' respectable pulpits and speak at anniversaries and the like. Each opportunity needs to be weighed on its merit, but the evangelist's calling is a unique one and his emphasis is to be rescuing the lost. C. T. Studd's little ditty is helpful here:

> Some like to sit within the sound
> Of church or chapel bell;
> I'd rather run a rescue shop
> Within a yard of hell.

There is a temptation to cultivate influential contacts without due attention to their spiritual pedigree. It cannot be right to give a platform to people merely because they have professional skills or are financially generous. Attention must be paid also to their spiritual qualities. This can apply equally to musicians or those giving their testimonies. Harm has been done to famous people, newly converted, who are catapulted to a platform and hailed as Christians before they have had time enough to become established in their new found faith. Their spiritual standing and state is the first priority.

I have found that if an evangelistic mission 'goes well', the Lord (rightly) gets the glory. If, on the other hand, the mission struggles, the evangelist gets the blame! An evangelist is judged by the fruit. This is a pressure which can lead the evangelist to compromise basic biblical principles to increase the crowds and the response. Manipulation of the listeners' emotions or massaging statistics is straightforward dishonesty. We all know that psychological pressure can apparently boost the numbers of people who respond, but such decisions are not only dishonest, they are harmful to those who feel they have tried Christianity, and found that 'it didn't work'. I have seen 'appeals' abused, prolonged and broadened so much that virtually all the congregation ought to have responded! If God is at work, we do not need to stoop to such methods. There should be integrity and humility in reporting responses – statistics should not be *evangelastic!*

We are doing God's work and must not be tempted to 'soften' the gospel, which by nature exposes sin and calls an individual to real discipleship. Paul was obviously aware of these temptations for he wrote:

> Therefore, since we have this ministry, as we have received mercy, we do not lose heart. But we have renounced the hidden things of shame, not walking in craftiness nor handling the word of God deceitfully, but by manifestation of the truth commending ourselves to every man's conscience in the sight of God. But even if our gospel is veiled, it is veiled to those who are perishing, whose minds the god of this age has blinded, who do not believe, lest the light of the gospel of the glory of Christ, who is the image of God, should shine on them. For we do not preach ourselves, but Christ Jesus the Lord, and ourselves your servants for Jesus' sake. (2 Cor. 4:1-5)

Even more forcefully Paul wrote 'But even if we, or an angel from heaven, should preach any gospel to you other than what we have preached to you, let him be accursed' (Gal. 1:8). Then Paul repeats: 'As we have said before, so now I say again, if anyone preaches any other gospel to you than what you have received, let him be accursed' (1:9).

However, if God uses the evangelist in a mighty way, then all the glory must be given to the Lord who alone can save men and women. The Lord will not share His glory with anyone else (Isa. 42:8; 48:11). When Corrie Ten Boom was thanked for her messages, she said she treated each expression of gratitude and praise as a rose, and then at the end of the day presented to the Lord a bouquet of roses. There are still people (including evangelists) like Diotrephes, who love to have the pre-eminence in the church (3 John:9). We need to be reminded that the Lord alone gives the increase, and if our work is blessed, it is the Lord's doing (Ps. 75:6; 1 Cor. 3:6-7). Bill Gothard says: 'I am responsible for the depth of my life, God is responsible for the breadth of my ministry.'

It is interesting that many evangelists leave their first calling and go into pastoral work, or even itinerant Bible teaching. It is not for me to question another person's calling and leading, but I wonder whether this move is because the pressure for results becomes too wearing. Undoubtedly, there is greater appreciation from believers when the Word is preached to them than when it is presented evangelistically; and perhaps ministry to Christians appears as an easier option than the cut and thrust of evangelism. In many denominational groupings, the pastor is treated with a greater esteem than the evangelist. Nevertheless, the evangelist is to remain true to his gift and calling, remembering that he is 'the prisoner of the Lord', and real joy comes in fulfilling that individual call. Others in the body of Christ can be of great encouragement urging on the evangelist.

WORK

Beware the peril of the pendulum. There is a danger of becoming either lazy, or a workaholic. The evangelist needs to lead a balanced life where deep devotion, earnest prayer and family hours are matched by a zeal to seek to reach unsaved people with the gospel.

I personally feel that the evangelist should work more hours than any secular worker. Too many evangelists claim to be full-time Christian workers, but in reality they are only doing the hours of someone who is part time. Samuel Chadwick, founder of the Methodist Cliff College, told his students, 'You cannot be an evangelist and anything else.' In Isaiah 5 the parable of the vineyard describes how the vine is only of value if it brings forth fruit. This is the calling of the evangelist. His labour is to be concentrated, and his attitude is to be professional without ever becoming 'a professional'. John Henry Jowitt never liked to hear the sound of workmen going to their employment early in the morning without him being in the study. After all, his was eternal work.

Long ago Chuck Swindoll made some promises before God which would be helpful to adapt in our situations:

I promise to keep doing original and hard work in my study. Those to whom I am called deserve my best efforts.

I promise to maintain a heart for God. That means I will pray frequently, and stay devoted to Him and my calling.

I promise to remain accountable. Living the life of a religious Lone Ranger is unbiblical; it's dangerous.

I promise to stay faithful to my family. My wife deserves my time, affection, and undivided attention. Our ... children deserve the same.

I promise to be who I am. Just me. I plan to keep laughing, saying things a little off the wall, being a friend, and making a few mistakes each month.

The evangelist is able to use his messages over and over again. The brusque Yorkshire evangelist, Herbert Silverwood, used to say, 'If you can't work out a new sermon, sole and heel an old one.' In my own experience, preaching over twenty times in a week, and sometimes as many as thirty-five times, there is no way that I could possibly prepare a new message each time. The Lord Jesus clearly repeated His messages and the apostle Paul gave his testimony fully three times in the book of Acts. John Wesley said, 'I don't get into a sermon until I have preached it forty times!' However, my sermons, which I regard as the tools of my trade, are the means I have to get across to the listening crowd the message of the gospel. My sermons must not lose their edge, but must be fresh, and delivered from a full heart that is on fire for the Lord. I find I need constantly to be preparing new messages for my own self-discipline and to maintain freshness both for myself and for my more regular hearers. I must not offer stale manna to people. A sermon is to be as a message from God for the listener, and therefore cannot be prepared hurriedly. An evangelist will have natural ability, but that talent cannot be relied upon to 'pull out of the hat another talk'. The evangelist must not settle for mediocrity, superficiality or fake spirituality. Change is a way of keeping fresh, so it is vital to vary our approach to preaching the gospel. We all learn from others, and pick up seed thoughts, insights and ideas; but although plagiarism may be a short cut, it is not the route to blessing.

The itinerant evangelist will find that the only thing which is regular about his life is its irregularity. Personally, I often find myself arriving home at two or three in the morning, having been travelling for hours since the last meeting. (My car often acts as my hotel, office, sanctuary and travelling companion.) Such a lifestyle is not conducive to a set time for the 'morning watch'. However, it is no excuse for ignoring it either. Whether living in others' homes or hotels, the time with God each day is the priority – more vital than any 'urgent' matter.

Travelling is tiring, as is meeting new people. We become more vulnerable to Satan's snares when we are physically weary (see 1 Kings 19). We are involved in a spiritual battle, and persuading and counselling can be gruelling work, but it is what we exist for. It is a privilege. It compares with no other task on earth. The temptation can be to do too much and suffer spiritual burnout. Vance Havner said, 'Those who do not come apart and rest awhile, come apart.' Again, a board of accountability can be a valued protector against extremes of work, or laziness. Work is no substitute for devotion, and laziness is no lifestyle for the evangelist. Again, integrity is the key theme. Paul writes in 2 Corinthians 2:14-17, 'Now thanks be to God who always leads us in triumph in Christ, and through us diffuses the fragrance of His knowledge in every place. For we are to God the fragrance of Christ among those who are being saved and among those who are perishing.'

DISCOURAGEMENT

Despite the image of an evangelist living in a blaze of glory and glamour, the truth is very often exactly the opposite. In the West, most evangelistic missions are not on the scale of a Billy Graham crusade, and are without any of the support staff. Many an evangelist is his own administrator, advance man, director of publicity, preacher, counsellor and follow up co-ordinator, and even director of music! The evangelist may well write and distribute his own tracts, drive his own car (as well as carrying out roadside repairs on it!), live quite modestly and spend well over half his married life away from home on the road. Whilst wanting to be a member of a particular local church back home, often the evangelist is not there and is unable to gain the many benefits of fellowship because of absences. This is a recipe for discouragement, disappointment and even, if one is not careful, bitterness. As a church has expectations of the evangelist, the evangelist has expectations of the inviting group of Christians. This too can lead to a sense of being let down. The evangelist's life can be a very lonely one despite the fact that one is constantly surrounded by crowds. If an evangelist can work in a team, it can be valuable to the ministry and to the people involved, but often lack of personnel and finance may prohibit this.

The pressure to do so much may mean the family back home is neglected; travelling may lead to a diet of junk food; and speed limits can become a nuisance! (Do I fear the police more than the Lord?) Cutting corners becomes so much a habit of life, one can forget that there even are corners. If the Christian life is anything, it is abundant because of its balance. We need evangelists who are balanced in each aspect of life and ministry.

A strong devotional life, being fed on the Word of God, and casting our cares upon the Lord will protect us in a large measure from the 'black dog' (as Winston Churchill described his times of weariness and discouragement). 'For consider Him who endured such hostility from sinners against Himself, lest you become weary and discouraged in your souls' (Heb. 12:3). There is no substitute for meeting with God. It helps us to be more aware of the ways of God, and also to understand ourselves better. We each have different personalities and temperaments, reacting differently to various situations. Paul wrote: 'But we have this treasure in earthen vessels, that the excellence of the power may be of God and not of us. We are hard pressed on every side, yet not crushed; we are perplexed, but not in despair; persecuted, but not forsaken; struck down, but not destroyed – always carrying about in the body the dying of the Lord Jesus, that the life of Jesus also may be manifested in our body' (2 Cor. 4:7-10).

COMFORTS AND ENCOURAGEMENT

Despite these issues, I can testify to the great joy of being an evangelist. I count it a real privilege to be able to devote all my waking hours to preparation for, or the actual proclaiming of the gospel. Happiness is not in my job description, but I find it is often a real bonus and perk of the job. It is thrilling to meet people who have been converted through evangelism, and it may be that the Lord keeps us from seeing all the fruit lest we become puffed up with pride. In times of pressure, the evangelist can remind himself of the certainty that the Lord called him to the task, just as Paul reminded Timothy of his calling (2 Tim. 1:6). Speaking personally, I have on occasions sought the Lord's mind as to whether I am to continue as an evangelist, but have always been driven to the sure conclusion that the Lord called me into this and I have no alternative, if I am to remain obedient.

God gives the grace for all he asks us to do. If I keep short accounts with the Lord, bringing my actions and reactions into submission to His will, I find joy. Jesus said: 'I am the vine, you are the branches. He who abides in Me, and I in him, bears much fruit; for without Me you can do nothing.... If you abide in Me, and My words abide in you, you will ask what you desire and it shall be done for you' (John 15:5, 7). There is no way out of suffering for the cause of Christ (2 Tim. 2:3-4; 3:12), but we have confidence both in the power of the gospel (2 Cor. 4:1-6) and in the faithfulness of God (2 Tim. 1:12).

For encouragement, memorize 1 Corinthians 1:27-29 and 2 Corinthians 1:3-6; 3:5, and keep 'looking unto Jesus, the author and finisher of our faith, who for the joy that was set before Him endured the cross, despising the shame, and has sat down at the right hand of the throne of God' (Heb. 12:2).

17 Problems, principles and parables for the evangelist

Prayer and evangelism are often the Cinderellas of Christian experience. In heaven, each person will be able to worship the Lord, sing His praises and serve Him, but will not be able to win souls. That wise work can be done only here and now. If as Christians we do not obey the Lord's command to go and preach to every creature while we are alive, it will be too late when we have died. It will be too late, also, for the unconverted. If this generation does not reach the lost, no other generation will be able to – their opportunity will have gone for ever.

One London preacher spoke of three problems or hindrances in evangelism. I hope I am not by nature a pessimist, but there are, it seems, at least *five* main problems that each Christian and certainly every evangelist faces in seeking to reach the lost effectively. However, to each of these problems there is a Bible principle and parable answering the issue.

THE FIRST ISSUE: THE PROBLEM OF WICKEDNESS

We live in an age of unprecedented evil. People can watch and witness terrible things, all of which desensitize their minds to moral or spiritual values. Apathy or antagonism to the gospel is often the order of the day. What one generation tolerates in moderation the next accepts in excess. The seeds sown thirty years ago are being reaped now.

The natural reaction is to be tempted to give up, feeling that people are too difficult to get alongside and too hard of heart if we do meet them. However, this is no reason to give up in despair. There is a Bible principle which actually ought to lead to great hope: 'Where sin abounded, grace abounded much more' (Rom. 5:20). Christ Jesus didn't come 'to call the righteous, but sinners, to repentance' (Matt. 9:13). Great wickedness, as well as hurting the heart of sensitive followers of Christ, should also be a reminder that these are the very people for whom Christ came into the world.

The Lord knows our situation. In the parable of the wheat and the weeds in Matthew 13:24-30, we read of the master's full awareness of the state of the field. He said, 'An enemy has done this' and, 'Let both grow together until the harvest' (vv. 28 and 30). Christ said of His commission, 'I send you out as sheep in the midst of wolves...' (Matt. 10:16), and Paul quoted Psalm 44:22, saying, 'For Your sake we are killed all day long; we are counted as sheep for the slaughter' (Rom. 8:36).

However, these people around us are our mission field. We love them because the Lord loves them. We have no monopoly on grace. Let us bear the heat of the day, because it may be that we will be used to reach some who throughout their lives have led lost, lousy lives, but who may be saved before it is too late (see Matt. 20:1-16). The Lord said to Jonah, 'And should I not pity Nineveh...?' (Jonah 4:11).

This attitude is well illustrated by John Wesley who wrote in his journal: 'We came to Newcastle about six; and after short refreshment, walked into the town. I was surprised: so much drunkenness, cursing and swearing (even from the mouths of little children), do I never remember to have seen and heard before in so small a compass of time. Surely this place is ripe for...' Our natural reaction would be to complete the sentence by words such as 'hell' or 'judgement', but Wesley saw things differently: 'Surely this place is ripe for Him Who came not to call the righteous but sinners to repentance' (Wesley's *Journals,* 28 May 1742).

William Booth, the founder of the Salvation Army, said, 'Go for sinners and go for the worst.' So much of our evangelistic effort is concentrated solely on the smallish percentage of the population who still have contact with the church, or us. Evangelism Explosion have successfully aimed at such people. However, what about those who spend their free time in clubs and pubs, who feel intimidated about going to church, who do not know our hymns or the books of the Bible? They need Christ, and He is still able to save them. The mark of a true work of God is when ordinary, working people are converted. Let us be encouraged by the Word of God to go and reach them.

THE SECOND ISSUE: THE PROBLEM OF WEAKNESS
We often feel that we neither have the resources nor the people to run massive evangelistic campaigns. The mass media, generally speaking, do not cover our work, and rarely show anything which we feel fairly represents the gospel. Think along these lines for any length of time and you can start to feel depressed. But God is still on the throne, and we know that He will build His church.

However, there is a Bible principle which is the antidote to any sense of despair: 'God has chosen the foolish things of the world to confound the things which are mighty.' The world looks for great talent, but God calls and then equips and uses to His glory, the person or work submitted to Him.

As a Christian gives away a tract, and tries to speak about Christ, what is happening? As far as the world is concerned, nothing much. But in passing on a tiny gospel seed, great things can be accomplished.

Let's not forget the parable of the mustard seed: 'The kingdom of heaven is like a mustard seed, which a man took and sowed in his field, which indeed is the least of all the seeds; but when it is grown it is greater than the herbs and becomes a tree, so that the birds of the air come and nest in its branches' (Matt. 13:31-32). God can use the smallest and weakest person or effort.

I am not arguing that we do things which are foolish *per se*, but that God will use the efforts of the witness or evangelist who is honestly aiming at reaching the lost and seeking to glorify God. If one method does not appear to be blessed, we should try others without compromising the truth or standard of the gospel.

THE THIRD ISSUE: THE PROBLEM OF WASTAGE

Every Sunday school teacher, tract distributor, or worker with the elderly fears that his or her faithful efforts are largely wasted. The evangelist can feel similar despondency and despair. We often hear that we are called to be faithful and not fruitful, and of course there is truth in that; but faithfulness and fruitfulness are often married to each other. Most testimonies include reference to childhood attendance at Sunday school, even if it was only for a few months. If gospel seed is sown, it will bring fruit in God's good time. Ecclesiastes 11:6 sets out a great principle:

> In the morning sow your seed,
> And in the evening do not withhold your hand;
> For you do not know which will prosper,

Either this or that,
Or whether both alike will be good.

The Lord in His life did not see great fruit, and the disciple is not going to be above the Master. There will always be losses, but how can one reap if there has been no sowing? Praying for revival is fine, as long as the earnest desire is not that there should be reaping without sowing, which is an excuse for laziness and a recipe for disappointment.

THE FOURTH ISSUE: THE PROBLEM OF WAITING
Satan exploits our desire to see immediate fruit, by making us feel that it is time to give up. How far from catching a shoal of fish were the discouraged disciples when they began gathering in their nets? Just the width of a fishing boat. The Lord gave fresh direction and what a catch! When Sir Winston Churchill went back to his school, Harrow, to speak his message to the scholars, his speech was as memorable as it was short. He said simply, 'Never, never, never, give up!' He then sat down. Evangelists need to learn that lesson.

But the Bible teaches a vital principle: 'And let us not grow weary while doing good, for in due season we shall reap if we do not lose heart' (Gal. 6:9).

In Judges 19 and 20 we read the appalling description of the multiple rape and abuse of the Levite's concubine. The Israelites gathered and sought God as to how they were to punish the Benjamites who were guilty of such depraved behaviour. The Lord clearly instructed them to go into battle against the tribe. In obedience they went twice...but were defeated. Only on the third occasion did they gain the victory. Why God allowed this I do not know, but they were being obedient. To break a boulder may take 1,000 blows. Are the first 999 wasted? Of course not! Efforts to reach lives which are hurting, hardened and held captive by Satan may appear to be wasted; but in God's economy they may be His method to bring a soul to life through the saving power of the Lord Jesus Christ.

Patience is needed in effective evangelism. Christ said, 'The kingdom of God is as if a man should scatter seed on the ground, and should sleep by night and rise by day, and the seed should spout and grow, he himself does not know how. For the earth yields crops by itself: first the blade, then the head, after that the full grain in the head. But when the grain ripens, immediately he puts in the sickle because the harvest has come' (Mark 4:26-29). Growth is a hidden, secret thing. But clearly, there is a divinely established order between labour and achievement; I can leave the rest to God, however, when I have done my duty – when He has pledged to do what I cannot, and when I do not understand the process of growth. Stuart Olyott, of Bryntirion Bible College in Wales, said, 'Almost all mistakes in Christians' work are caused by impatience.'

THE FIFTH ISSUE: THE PROBLEM OF WILLINGNESS

I suspect that this is the real problem, and it lies with us. Following the Lord Jesus, being made into fishers of men, seeking to rescue the perishing, and by all means reaching some, is never easy. The work of the evangelist is not hit and run, nor hit and miss. Christ did not promise that working for Him would be straightforward. A regular routine of church services, not disturbed by new converts with their numerous problems, is an easier option than making our churches into rescue shops for those living without hope in this world or the next.

Evangelism should be at the top of our personal and church agendas. Are we prepared to pray and to fast with earnestness, pleading for those who never pray for themselves?

Are we, like the apostle Paul, able to say that we are innocent of the blood of all men (Acts 20:26)? Poussa the potter, after many efforts to make a porcelain set for the Emperor's table, despairing of making anything worthy of a king's acceptance, flung himself into the furnace, where he was glazing master-pieces, with the intention of intensifying the heat. How much of ourselves are we willing to give to reach men and women?

I was greatly challenged by an elderly Lebanon Evangelical Mission worker, Miss Fitzpatrick. After fifty years of missionary service, she retired to the Isle of Wight. In her late eighties, she would stand at the gate to her house and ask passing holidaymakers if they would like to come and see her garden. 'But when we were in the garden, we would talk about more important matters,' she told me. I visited her in Ryde Hospital after she had had a bad fall. We talked a while, then I prayed with her. Just before I left she gripped my hand and with tears in her eyes said, 'Roger, please pray for me. I've been here for three months now and not yet won a soul to Christ, and I don't know what is wrong.' I felt very challenged that I allow months to go by without feeling that concern.

There is a Bible principle and parable here. Jesus said, 'Unless a grain of wheat falls into the ground and dies, it remains alone, but if it dies it produces much grain. He who loves his life will lose it and he who hates his life in this world will keep it for eternal life' (John 12:24-25).

I would beg of us all that we come before the Lord in our church prayer meetings and in our individual quiet times, to rededicate ourselves to the task of evangelism, and then with others urgently decide on a systematic, prayerful plan of action to reach the lost, whatever the cost.

> All my days and all my hours;
> All my will and all my powers;
> Not a fraction but the whole;
> Shall be Thine, dear Lord.

18

'And sow to reap': An exposition for evangelists, about evangelism

'Everybody is ignorant,' said Will Rogers, 'only on different subjects.'

The preacher in Ecclesiastes 11 describes our ignorance of the works of God and of the future. In particular we do not know which seeds will germinate and produce fruit (11:6). This should be our incentive to be about the work of sowing. The evangelist has the privilege of scattering the gospel message. We do not know which word spoken to a neighbour, shopkeeper or colleague will be used by God. We do not know how a tract will be used or even where it will end up. Therefore, let us be sowers wherever we go.

Ecclesiastes 11:1-6 develops this theme and its teaching can be divided into eight helpful sections.

1. SOW EXPECTING TO REAP

Cast your bread upon the waters,
for you will find it after many days (Eccles. 11:1) .

Though this well-known proverb is difficult to explain, the lesson itself is clear. Instead of living self-indulgently, we should live to give away the gospel message. As we share the gospel, we have God's promise: 'in due season we shall reap if we do not lose heart' (Gal. 6:9).

Reaping is the natural result of sowing. If no souls have been saved by our witness for some time, we should not give up. Rather, we should search our own hearts and carry on. As Warren Wiersbe so often says: 'It is always too soon to quit.' There is a story of a discouraged young preacher who approached C. H. Spurgeon. Spurgeon is supposed to have replied, 'Well, you don't expect to see converts every week, do you?' 'No!', replied the young man. 'Well, that is why you don't,' said Spurgeon!

Count Zinzendorf founded the 'Order of the Grain of Mustard-Seed'. Its simple principle was that every member should seek daily the conversion of some other soul.

Let us speak to the lost about the Christ who died for them. Let us ask the Lord for fruit – and expect it.

2. SOW GENEROUSLY

Give a serving to seven, and also to eight (Eccles 11:2).

This is the preacher's quaint way of saying that if we have seven opportunities we should take them all, and if we meet with an eighth, take that as well and eight more if we can!

I have always admired those who can turn any situation into an opportunity. An evangelist was asked by a stranger, 'Can you change a coin?' As he did, he commented, 'My trouble is that all

I can do is change money, but I have a Friend who can change your life...'

The emphasis today is to wait for the opportunity to witness. For those we constantly meet, I am sure that this is right. In answer to prayer, God will give the right moment and opening. However, what about those we meet only once? Surely we have an obligation to sow the seed in their hearts as well! On 8 June 1741, John Wesley wrote in his journal:

> For these two days I had made an experiment which I had been so often and earnestly pressed to do – speaking to none concerning the things of God unless my heart was free to it. And what was the result? Why –
>
> (1) that I spoke to none at all for fourscore miles together; no, not even to him that travelled with me in the chaise, unless a few words at first setting out;
>
> (2) that I had no cross either to bear or to take up, and commonly, in an hour or two, fell fast asleep;
>
> (3) that I had much respect shown me wherever I came, everyone behaving to me as to a civil, good-natured gentleman. Oh, how pleasing is all this to flesh and blood! Need ye 'compass sea and land' to make 'proselytes' to this?

May we never go anywhere without our hearts prepared, tracts or booklets ready, and being prayerfully eager to speak about the Saviour to all who cross our path.

3. SOW WHILE THERE IS OPPORTUNITY

> For you do not know what evil will be on the earth.
> If the clouds are full of rain,
> They empty themselves upon the earth (Eccles. 11:2, 3).

The need is urgent. Christ has died and risen. He is the only way to God, salvation and heaven. Only we have the opportunity to witness to our generation – no-one else can. Jesus said, 'The harvest is ready' – to reap, or to rot!

The verse says that the very purpose of clouds is to empty themselves. As Christians our *raison d'être* is to serve Christ and speak of Him. C. M. Alexander put it very bluntly: 'Anyone who is not doing personal work has sin in his life; I don't care who you are – preacher, teacher, mother, father, son – if you are not leading definite people to a definite Saviour at a definite time, or trying hard to do so, you have sin in your life.'

4. SOW WHERE YOU ARE

If a tree falls to the south or the north,
In the place where the tree falls, there it shall lie (Eccles. 11:3).

It is easy to think that if only we were in a different place, then there would be better opportunities (the greener-grass syndrome). This attitude only leads to despondency. In contrast, the apostle Paul, when imprisoned, did not see himself as Caesar's prisoner, but instead wrote, 'I, Paul, a prisoner of the Lord.' If we are hemmed in, then we are there for God's purpose. Just like trees fallen in a particular place, God has deliberately put us where we are to influence others.

An old people's home, a works canteen, a factory floor, outside a school gate, in a car or a hospital bed, are all places where we can witness.

Inviting a friend for coffee, giving a tract to someone you meet, writing a letter which shares the faith with a relative, or giving an evangelistic book, are all ways of sowing the gospel seed.

5. SOWING DESPITE THE DIFFICULTIES

He who observes the wind will not sow,
And he who regards the clouds will not reap (Eccles. 11:4).

There are always reasons or excuses for not getting on with the great job of evangelism. The place for effective evangelism is not always in a cosy room or sitting on a soft cushion. You cannot change the world from a desk; you need to be in constant contact with people.

> Must I be carried to the skies
> On flowery beds of ease,
> While others fought to win the prize
> And sailed through raging seas?

True zeal disregards the cost and consequences of taking up the cross to follow the Christ who bled in order to bless. Wherever there is reaping, the hard work of sowing has been done first. Labour and reward are permanently linked in nature and evangelism. At the time, sowing may seem unrewarding as harvest is so many months away; but how can we expect to reap if there has been no sowing?

Although the media and educational systems are not sowing the good seed as we would like them to, that is no excuse for us to give up. Instead, it is a further impetus for us to do the work which is our calling anyway.

We will constantly meet and talk with those who have never been to a Sunday school or church, and have never read the Bible. They may not believe or even want to. They may not believe there is absolute truth at all. To begin with, the ground may be hard, but, with our prayers, we plough and continue sowing.

6. SOW, TRUSTING GOD TO DO HIS UNSEEN WORK

> As you do not know what is the way of the wind,
> Or how the bones grow in the womb of her who is with child,
> So you do not know the works of God who makes all things.
> (Eccles. 11:5)

What can a few words of the gospel accomplish when the people we speak to hear millions of other words in their lives? What can one tract achieve when the recipient reads books, newspapers and magazines by the hundred? Humanly speaking, nothing, except that God has chosen us to scatter the message of salvation to people who are lost.

As we do not fully understand human conception and growth, so we cannot understand the work of God in the soul of man. It is a miracle. Every time a seed grows to produce a harvest, God is taking a weak thing to do a mighty work. Do we feel that God could never use us? How wrong we are! It gives God pleasure to save precious souls through what many regard as weak, foolish or a mere stumbling-block.

In the early hours of a morning I picked up an American hitchhiker whom I spoke to about the Lord, only to find I was the third Christian in the UK to do so. I passed on an evangelistic booklet. Some time later, I received a postcard with a Swiss postmark from that hitchhiker. In it he shared how the person had been converted, met with more Christians in France, and enrolled at L'Abri Bible School for a year. I was just sowing and watering the seed; God was doing this unseen work of giving the increase.

7. SOW AT ALL TIMES

> In the morning sow your seed,
> And in the evening do not withhold your hand;
> For you do not know which will prosper,
> Either this or that,
> Or whether both alike will be good. (Eccles. 11:6)

There is a morning and an evening to every day. There is also a morning and evening to every life. At all times of the day we are to sow. Whether it is convenient or not, we are to sow.

At all times of life, we are to sow. Personal work is not just for the young evangelist; it is for all. A retired missionary couple I know are still very faithful in praying for all the villages in their vicinity. They still visit many homes regularly, distribute Christian literature, open up their house to young people and talk to all. Like Caleb, age is not going to cause them to cease from their calling.

D. L. Moody, who never let a day go by without speaking to somebody about Christ, was called 'Crazy Moody', because he was so keen to give away tracts in Chicago.

In describing his first acts of service, C. H. Spurgeon wrote:

> I used to write texts on little scraps of paper and drop them anywhere that some poor creatures might pick them up and receive them as messages of mercy to their souls. I could scarcely content myself even for five minutes without trying to do something for Christ. If I walked along the street I must have a few tracts with me; if I went into a railway carriage, I must drop a tract out of the window; if I had a moment's leisure I must be upon my knees or at my Bible; if I were in company, I must turn the subject of conversation to Christ, that I might serve my Master.

Surely Christ's love for us and ours for Him, will spur us on as evangelists to continue to make Christ known.

There are many things we do not know, but we *do know that we are commanded to go into all the world and preach the gospel*. As we do the work of evangelists, we know God will bless and use us.

May we every day discover afresh the joy of sowing and being a witness or an evangelist.

Appendix

THE AMSTERDAM AFFIRMATIONS
When the Billy Graham Evangelistic Association met for their International Conference for Itinerant Evangelists in Amsterdam, in 1983 and 1986, they devised a series of 'Affirmations' for evangelists. They are very helpful, and summarize the responsibilities that evangelists take upon themselves when following the Lord's call into evangelistic work. There are fifteen statements in all, as follows:

I. We confess Jesus Christ as God, our Lord and Saviour, who is revealed in the Bible, which is the infallible Word of God.

II. We affirm our commitment to the Great Commission of our Lord, and we declare our willingness to go anywhere, do anything, and sacrifice anything God requires of us in the fulfilment of that Commission.

III. We respond to God's call to the biblical ministry of the evangelist, and accept our solemn responsibility to preach the Word to all peoples as God gives opportunity.

IV. God loves every human being, who, apart from faith in Christ, is under God's judgement and destined for hell.

V. The heart of the biblical message is the good news of God's salvation, which comes by grace alone through faith in the risen Lord Jesus Christ and his atoning death on the cross for our sins.

VI. In our proclamation of the gospel, we recognize the urgency of calling all to decision to follow Jesus Christ as Lord and Saviour, and to do so without coercion or manipulation.

VII. We need and desire to be filled and controlled by the Holy Spirit as we bear witness to the gospel of Jesus Christ, because God alone can turn sinners from their sin and bring them to everlasting life.

VIII. We acknowledge our obligation, as servants of God, to lead lives of holiness and moral purity, knowing that we exemplify Christ to the church and the world.

IX. A life of regular and faithful prayer and Bible study is essential to our personal spiritual growth, and to our power for ministry.

X. We will be faithful stewards of all that God gives us, and will be accountable to others in the finances of our ministry, and honest in our reporting of statistics.

XI. Our families are a responsibility given to us by God, and are a sacred trust to be kept as faithfully as our call to minister to others.

XII. We are responsible to the church, and will endeavour always to conduct our ministries so as to build up the local body of believers and serve the church at large.

XIII. We are responsible to arrange for the spiritual care of those who come to faith under our ministry, to encourage them to identify with the local body of believers, and seek to provide for the instruction of believers in witnessing to the gospel.

XIV. We share Christ's deep concern for the personal and social sufferings of humanity, and we accept our responsibility as Christians and as evangelists to do our utmost to alleviate human need.

XV. We beseech the body of Christ to join with us in prayer and work for peace in our world, for revival and a renewed dedication to the biblical priority of evangelism in the church, and for the oneness of believers in Christ for the fulfilment of the Great Commission, until Christ returns.

Select Bibliography

Paul Bassett, *God's Way*, Ambassador Publications, 1981.

Phillips Brooks, *The Joy of Preaching* (Previously *Lectures on Preaching*), Kregel Publications, 1907.

Roger Carswell, *Growing Through Encouragement*, Bryntirion Press, 1997.

Roger Carswell, *How Small a Whisper*, Baker Book House, 1989.

Arnold Dallimore, *George Whitefield*, Vols 1 & 2, Banner of Truth, 1970 and 1980.

Phil Downer, *Eternal Impact*, Harvest House, 1997.

Billy Graham, *A Biblical Standard for Evangelists*, World Wide Publications, 1984.

Sterling Huston, *The Billy Graham Crusade Handbook*, World Wide Publications, 1981.

Trevor F. Knight, *God's Early Evangelists*, Young Life, 1996.

David L. Larsen, *The Company of Preachers*, Kregel Publications, 1998.

David L. Larsen, *The Evangelism Mandate*, Crossway Books, 1992.

Kenneth Prior, *The Gospel in a Pagan Society*, Christian Focus, 1995.

James Rye, *The Communicator's Craft*, IVP, 1990.

J. C. Ryle, *Christian Leaders of the Eighteenth Century*, Banner of Truth, 1885.

J. O. Sanders, *Effective Evangelism*, Christian Focus, 1999.

C. H. Spurgeon, *Lectures to my Students*, Christian Focus, 1998.

Roger Steer, *A Man in Christ*, OMF, 1990.

John Stott, ed. *Making Christ Known: Historic Mission Documents from the Lausanne Movement, 1974-1989* (Grand Rapids, Michigan: Eerdmans, 1996).

Jerry Vines, *A Guide to Effective Sermon Delivery*, Moody Press, 1986.

Warren Wiersbe, *Listening to the Giants*, Baker Book House, 1980.

——————— *On Being a Servant of God*, Nelson, 1993.

——————— *Preaching and Teaching with Imagination*, Victor Books, 1994.

——————— *The Integrity Crisis*, Oliver-Nelson, 1998.